THE RELIGION OF

BABYLONIA AND ASSYRIA

The Lord God Enki

BY

THEOPHILUS G. PINCHES, LL.D.

Published by

The Jaredite Publication Society

THE RELIGION OF THE BABYLONIANS AND ASSYRIANS

CHAPTER I

FOREWORD

Position, and Period.

The religion of the Babylonians and Assyrians was the polytheistic faith professed by the peoples inhabiting the Tigris and Euphrates valleys from what may be regarded as the dawn of history until the Christian era began, or, at least, until the inhabitants were brought under the influence of Christianity. The chronological period covered may be roughly estimated at about 5000 years. The belief of the people, at the end of that time, being Babylonian heathenism leavened with Judaism, the country was probably ripe for the reception of the new faith. Christianity, however, by no means replaced the earlier polytheism, as is evidenced by the fact, that the worship of Nebo and the gods associated with him continued until the fourth century of the Christian era.

By whom followed.

It was the faith of two distinct peoples—the Sumero-Akkadians, and the Assyro-Babylonians. In what country it had its beginnings is unknown—it comes before us, even at the earliest period, as a faith already well-developed, and from that fact, as well as from the names of the numerous deities, it is clear that it began with the former race—the Sumero-Akkadians—who spoke a non-Semitic language largely affected by phonetic decay, and in which the grammatical forms had in certain cases become confused to such an extent that those who study it ask themselves whether the people who spoke it were able to understand each other without recourse to devices such as the "tones" to which the Chinese resort. With few exceptions, the names of the gods which the inscriptions reveal to us are all derived from this non-Semitic language, which furnishes us with satisfactory etymologies for such names as Merodach, Nergal, Sin, and the divinities mentioned in Berosus and

1

Damascius, as well as those of hundreds of deities revealed to us by the tablets and slabs of Babylonia and Assyria.

The documents.

Outside the inscriptions of Babylonia and Assyria, there is but little bearing upon the religion of those countries, the most important fragment being the extracts from Berosus and Damascius referred to above. Among the Babylonian and Assyrian remains, however, we have an extensive and valuable mass of material, dating from the fourth or fifth millennium before Christ until the disappearance of the Babylonian system of writing about the beginning of the Christian era. The earlier inscriptions are mostly of the nature of records, and give information about the deities and the religion of the people in the course of descriptions of the building and rebuilding of temples, the making of offerings, the performance of ceremonies, etc. Purely religious inscriptions are found near the end of the third millennium before Christ, and occur in considerable numbers, either in the original Sumerian text, or in translations, or both, until about the third century before Christ. Among the more recent inscriptions—those from the library of the Assyrian king Aššur-bani-âpli and the later Babylonian temple archives,—there are many lists of deities, with numerous identifications with each other and with the heavenly bodies, and explanations of their natures. It is needless to say that all this material is of enormous value for the study of the religion of the Babylonians and Assyrians, and enables us to reconstruct at first hand their mythological system, and note the changes which took place in the course of their long national existence. Many interesting and entertaining legends illustrate and supplement the information given by the bilingual lists of gods, the bilingual incantations and hymns, and the references contained in the historical and other documents. A trilingual list of gods enables us also to recognize, in some cases, the dialectic forms of their names.

The importance of the subject.

Of equal antiquity with the religion of Egypt, that of Babylonia and Assyria possesses some marked differences as to its development.

Beginning among the non-Semitic Sumero-Akkadian population, it maintained for a long time its uninterrupted development, affected mainly by influences from within, namely, the homogeneous local cults which acted and reacted upon each other. The religious systems of other nations did not greatly affect the development of the early non-Semitic religious system of Babylonia. A time at last came, however, when the influence of the Semitic inhabitants of Babylonia and Assyria was not to be gainsaid, and from that moment, the development of their religion took another turn. In all probably this augmentation of Semitic religious influence was due to the increased numbers of the Semitic population, and at the same period the Sumero-Akkadian language began to give way to the Semitic idiom which they spoke. When at last the Semitic Babylonian language came to be used for official documents, we find that, although the non-Semitic divine names are in the main preserved, a certain number of them have been displaced by the Semitic equivalent names, such as Šamaš for the sun-god, with Kittu and Mêšaru ("justice and righteousness") his attendants; Nabú ("the teacher" = Nebo) with his consort Tašmêtu ("the hearer"); Addu, Adad, or Dadu, and Rammanu, Ramimu, or Ragimu = Hadad or Rimmon ("the thunderer"); Bêl and Bêltu (Beltis = "the lord" and "the lady" /par excellence/), with some others of inferior rank. In place of the chief divinity of each state at the head of each separate pantheon, the tendency was to make Merodach, the god of the capital city Babylon, the head of the pantheon, and he seems to have been universally accepted in Babylonia, like Aššur in Assyria, about 2000 B.C. or earlier.

The uniting of two pantheons.

We thus find two pantheons, the Sumero-Akkadian with its many gods, and the Semitic Babylonian with its comparatively few, united, and forming one apparently homogeneous whole. But the creed had taken a fresh tendency. It was no longer a series of small, and to a certain extent antagonistic, pantheons composed of the chief god, his consort, attendants, children, and servants, but a pantheon of considerable extent, containing all the elements of the primitive but smaller pantheons, with a number of great gods who had raised Merodach to be their king.

3

In Assyria.

Whilst accepting the religion of Babylonia, Assyria nevertheless kept herself distinct from her southern neighbor by a very simple device, by placing at the head of the pantheon the god Aššur, who became for her the chief of the gods, and at the same time the emblem of her distinct national aspirations—for Assyria had no intention whatever of casting in her lot with her southern neighbor Nevertheless, Assyria possessed, along with the language of Babylonia, all the literature of that country—indeed, it is from the libraries of her kings that we obtain the best copies of the Babylonian religious texts, treasured and preserved by her with all the veneration of which her religious mind was capable,—and the religious fervor of the Oriental in most cases leaves that of the European, or at least of the ordinary Briton, far behind.

The later period in Assyria.

Assyria went to her downfall at the end of the seventh century before Christ worshiping her national god Aššur, whose cult did not cease with the destruction of her national independence. In fact, the city of Aššur, the center of that worship, continued to exist for a considerable period; but for the history of the religion of Assyria, as preserved there, we wait for the result of the excavations being carried on by the Germans, should they be fortunate enough to obtain texts belonging to the period following the fall of Nineveh.

In Babylonia.

Babylonia, on the other hand, continued the even tenor of her way. More successful at the end of her independent political career than her northern rival had been, she retained her faith, and remained the unswerving worshiper of Merodach, the great god of Babylon, to whom her priests attributed yet greater powers, and with whom all the other gods were to all appearance identified. This tendency to monotheism, however, never reached the culminating point—never became absolute —except, naturally, in the minds of those who, dissociating themselves, for philosophical reasons, from the superstitious teaching of the priests of Babylonia, decided for themselves that there was but one God, and worshiped Him. That orthodox Jews at that period may have found, in consequence of this monotheistic tendency, converts, is not by any means improbable—indeed, the names met with during the later period imply that converts to Judaism were made.

The picture presented by the study.

Thus we see, from the various inscriptions, both Babylonian and Assyrian—the former of an extremely early period—the growth and development, with at least one branching off, of one of the most important religious systems of the ancient world. It is not so important for modern religion as the development of the beliefs of the Hebrews, but as the creed of the people from which the Hebrew nation sprang, and from which, therefore, it had its beginnings, both corporeal and spiritual, it is such as no student of modern religious systems can afford to neglect. Its legends, and therefore its teachings, as will be seen in these pages, ultimately permeated the Semitic West, and may in some cases even had penetrated Europe, not only through heathen Greece, but also through the early Christians, who, being so many centuries nearer the time of the Assyro-Babylonians, and also nearer the territory which they anciently occupied, than we are, were far better acquainted than the people of the present day with the legends and ideas which they possessed.

Assyrian troops return after victory.

Head of Winged Bull

Photo: William Henry Goodyear

CHAPTER II

THE RELIGION OF THE BABYLONIANS AND ASSYRIANS

The Sumero-Akkadians and the Semites.

For the history of the development of the religion of the Babylonians and Assyrians much naturally depends upon the composition of the population of early Babylonia. There is hardly any doubt that the Sumero-Akkadians were non-Semites of a fairly pure race, but the country of their origin is still unknown, though a certain relationship with the Mongolian and Turkish nationalities, probably reaching back many centuries—perhaps thousands of years—before the earliest accepted date, may be regarded as equally likely. Equally uncertain is the date of the entry of the Semites, whose language ultimately displaced the non-Semitic Sumero-Akkadian idioms, and whose kings finally ruled over the land. During the third millennium before Christ Semites, bearing Semitic names, and called Amorites, appear, and probably formed the last considerable stratum of tribes of that race which entered the land. The name Martu, the Sumero-Akkadian equivalent of Amurru, "Amorite", is of frequent occurrence also before this period. The eastern Mediterranean coast district, including Palestine and the neighboring tracts, was known by the Babylonians and Assyrians as the land of the Amorites, a term which stood for the West in general even when these regions no longer bore that name. The Babylonians maintained their claim to sovereignty over that part as long as they possessed the power to do so, and naturally exercised considerable influence there. The existence in Palestine, Syria, and the neighboring states, of creeds containing the names of many Babylonian divinities is therefore not to be wondered at, and the presence of West Semitic divinities in the religion of the Babylonians need not cause us any surprise.

The Babylonian script and its evidence.

In consequence of the determinative prefix for a god or a goddess being, in the oldest form, a picture of an eight-rayed star, it has been assumed that Assyro-Babylonian mythology is, either wholly or

7

partly, astral in origin. This, however, is by no means certain, the character for "star" in the inscriptions being a combination of three such pictures, and not a single sign. The probability therefore is, that the use of the single star to indicate the name of a divinity arises merely from the fact that the character in question stands for /ana/, "heaven." Deities were evidently thus distinguished by the Babylonians because they regarded them as inhabitants of the realms above—indeed, the heavens being the place where the stars are seen, a picture of a star was the only way of indicating heavenly things. That the gods of the Babylonians were in many cases identified with the stars and planets is certain, but these identifications seem to have taken place at a comparatively late date. An exception has naturally to be made in the case of the sun and moon, but the god Merodach, if he be, as seems certain, a deified Babylonian king, must have been identified with the stars which bear his name after his worshipers began to pay him divine honors as the supreme deity, and naturally what is true for him may also be so for the other gods whom they worshiped The identification of some of the deities with stars or planets is, moreover, impossible, and if Êa, the god of the deep, and Anu, the god of the heavens, have their representatives among the heavenly bodies, this is probably the result of later development.[1]

Ancestor and hero-worship. The deification of kings.

Though there is no proof that ancestor-worship in general prevailed at any time in Babylonia, it would seem that the worship of heroes and prominent men was common, at least in early times. The tenth chapter of Genesis tells us of the story of Nimrod, who cannot be any other than

---

1 If there be any historical foundation for the statement that Merodach arranged the sun, the moon, the planets, and the stars, assigning to them their proper places and duties—a tradition which would make him the founder of the science of astronomy during his life upon earth—this, too, would tend to the probability that the origin of the gods of the Babylonians was not astral, as has been suggested, but that their identification with the heavenly bodies was introduced during the period of his reign.

the Merodach of the Assyro-Babylonian inscriptions; and other examples, occurring in semi-mythological times, are /En-we-dur-an-ki/, the Greek Edoreschos, and /Gilgameš/, the Greek Gilgamos, though Aelian's story of the latter does not fit in with the account as given by the inscriptions. In later times, the divine prefix is found before the names of many a Babylonian ruler—Sargon of Agadé,[2] Dungi of Ur (about 2500 B.C.), Rim-Sin or Eri-Aku (Arioch of Ellasar, about 2100 B.C.), and others. It was doubtless a kind of flattery to deify and pay these rulers divine honors during their lifetime, and on account of this, it is very probable that their godhood was utterly forgotten, in the case of those who were strictly historical, after their death. The deification of the kings of Babylonia and Assyria is probably due to the fact, that they were regarded as the representatives of God upon earth, and being his chief priests as well as his offspring (the personal names show that it was a common thing to regard children as the gifts of the gods whom their father worshiped), the divine fatherhood thus attributed to them naturally could, in the case of those of royal rank, give them a real claim to divine birth and honors An exception is the deification of the Babylonian Noah, Ut-napištim, who, as the legend of the Flood relates, was raised and made one of the gods by Aa or Ea, for his faithfulness after the great catastrophe, when he and his wife were translated to the "remote place at the mouth of the rivers." The hero Gilgameš, on the other hand, was half divine by birth, though it is not exactly known through whom his divinity came.

The earliest form of the Babylonian religion.

The state of development to which the religious system of the Babylonians had attained at the earliest period to which the inscriptions refer naturally precludes the possibility of a trustworthy history of its origin and early growth. There is no doubt, however, that it may be regarded as having reached the stage at which we find it in consequence of there being a number of states in ancient Babylonia (which was at that time like the Heptarchy in England) each possessing

---

2 According to Nabonidus's date 3800 B.C., though many Assyriologists regard this as being a millennium too early.

its own divinity—who, in its district, was regarded as supreme—with a number of lesser gods forming his court. It was the adding together of all these small pantheons which ultimately made that of Babylonia as a whole so exceedingly extensive. Thus the chief divinity of Babylon, as has already been stated, as Merodach; at Sippar and Larsa the sun-god Šamaš was worshiped; at Ur the moon-god Sin or Nannar; at Erech and Dêr the god of the heavens, Anu; at Muru, Ennigi, and Kakru, the god of the atmosphere, Hadad or Rimmon; at Êridu, the god of the deep, Aa or Êa; at Niffur[3] the god Bel; at Cuthah the god of war, Nergal; at Dailem the god Uraš; at Kiš the god of battle, Zagaga; Lugal-Amarda, the king of Marad, as the city so called; at Opis Zakar, one of the gods of dreams; at Agadé, Nineveh, and Arbela, Ištar, goddess of love and of war; Nina at the city Nina in Babylonia, etc. When the chief deities were masculine, they were naturally all identified with each other, just as the Greeks called the Babylonian Merodach by the name of Zeus; and as Zer-panîtum, the consort of Merodach, was identified with Juno, so the consorts, divine attendants, and children of each chief divinity, as far as they possessed them, could also be regarded as the same, though possibly distinct in their different attributes.

How the religion of the Babylonians developed.

The fact that the rise of Merodach to the position of king of the gods was due to the attainment, by the city of Babylon, of the position of capital of all Babylonia, leads one to suspect that the kingly rank of his father Êa, at an earlier period, was due to a somewhat similar cause, and if so, the still earlier kingship of Anu, the god of the heavens, may be in like manner explained. This leads to the question whether the first state to attain to supremacy was Dêr, Anu's seat, and whether Dêr was succeeded by Êridu, of which city Êa was the patron—concerning the importance of Babylon, Merodach's city, later on, there is no doubt whatever. The rise of Anu and Êa to divine overlordship, however, may not have been due to the political supremacy of the cities where they

---

3 Noufar at present, according to the latest explorers. Layard (1856) has Niffer, Loftus (1857) Niffar. The native spelling is Noufer, due to the French system of phonetics.

10

were worshiped—it may have come about simply on account of renown gained through religious enthusiasm due to wonders said to have been performed where they were worshiped, or to the reported discovery of new records concerning their temples, or to the influence of some renowned high-priest, like En-we-dur-an-ki of Sippar, whose devotion undoubtedly brought great renown to the city of his dominion.

Was Animism its original form?

But the question naturally arises, can we go back beyond the indications of the inscriptions? The Babylonians attributed life, in certain not very numerous cases, to such things as trees and plants, and naturally to the winds, and the heavenly bodies. Whether they regarded stones, rocks, mountains, storms, and rain in the same way, however, is doubtful, but it may be taken for granted, that the sea, with all its rivers and streams, was regarded as animated with the spirit of Êa and his children, whilst the great cities and temple-towers were pervaded with the spirit of the god whose abode they were. Innumerable good and evil spirits were believed in, such as the spirit of the mountain, the sea, the plain, and the grave. These spirits were of various kinds, and bore names which do not always reveal their real character—such as the /edimmu/, /utukku/, /šêdu/, /ašakku/ (spirit of fevers), /namtaru/ (spirit of fate), /âlû/ (regarded as the spirit of the south wind), /gallu/, /rabisu/, /labartu/, /labasu/, /ahhazu/ (the seizer), /lilu/ and /lilithu/ (male and female spirits of the mist), with their attendants.

All this points to animism as the pervading idea of the worship of the peoples of the Babylonian states in the prehistoric period—the attribution of life to every appearance of nature. The question is, however, Is the evidence of the inscriptions sufficient to make this absolutely certain? It is hard to believe that such intelligent people, as the primitive Babylonians naturally were, believed that such things as stones, rocks, mountains, storms, and rain were, in themselves, and apart from the divinity which they regarded as presiding over them, living things. A stone might be a /bît îli/ or bethel—a "house of god," and almost invested with the status of a living thing, but that does not prove that the Babylonians thought of every stone as being endowed with life, even in prehistoric times. Whilst, therefore, there are traces of a belief similar to that which an animistic creed might be regarded as possessing, it must be admitted that these seemingly animistic doctrines may have originated in another way, and be due to later developments. The power of the gods to create living things naturally makes possible the belief that they had also power to endow with a soul, and therefore with life and intelligence, any seemingly inanimate object. Such was probably the nature of Babylonian animism, if it may be so called. The legend of Tiawthu (Tiawath) may with great probability be regarded as the remains of a primitive animism which was the creed of the original and comparatively uncivilized Babylonians, who saw in the sea the producer and creator of all the monstrous shapes which are found therein; but any development of this idea in other directions was probably cut short by the priests, who must have realized, under the influence of the doctrine of the divine rise to perfection, that animism in general was altogether incompatible with the creed which they professed.

Image-worship and Sacred Stones.

Whether image-worship was original among the Babylonians and Assyrians is uncertain, and improbable; the tendency among the people in early times being to venerate sacred stones and other inanimate objects. As has been already pointed out, the {diopetres} of the Greeks was probably a meteorite, and stones marking the position of the Semitic bethels were probably, in their origin, the same. The boulders which were sometimes used for boundary-stones may have been the representations of these meteorites in later times, and it is noteworthy that the Sumerian group for "iron," /an-bar/, implies that the early Babylonians only knew of that metal from meteoric ironstone. The name of the god Nirig or Ênu-rêštu (Ninip) is generally written with the same group, implying some kind of connection between the two— the god and the iron. In a well-known hymn to that deity certain stones are mentioned, one of them being described as the "poison-tooth"[4] coming forth on the mountain, recalling the sacred rocks at Jerusalem

---

4 So called, probably, not because it sent forth poison, but on account of its likeness to a serpent's fang.

12

and Mecca. Boundary-stones in Babylonia were not sacred objects except in so far as they were sculptured with the signs of the gods.[5] With regard to the Babylonian bethels, very little can be said, their true nature being uncertain, and their number, to all appearance, small. Gifts were made to them, and from this fact it would seem that they were temples—true "houses of god," in fact—probably containing an image of the deity, rather than a stone similar to those referred to in the Old Testament.

Idols.

With the Babylonians, the gods were represented by means of stone images at a very early date, and it is possible that wood was also used. The tendency of the human mind being to attribute to the Deity a human form, the Babylonians were no exception to the rule. Human thoughts and feelings would naturally accompany the human form with which the minds of men endowed them. Whether the gross human passions attributed to the gods of Babylonia in Herodotus be of early date or not is uncertain—a late period, when the religion began to degenerate, would seem to be the more probable.

The adoration of sacred objects.

It is probable that objects belonging to or dedicated to deities were not originally worshiped—they were held as divine in consequence of their being possessed or used by a deity, like the bow of Merodach, placed in the heavens as a constellation, etc. The cities where the gods dwelt on earth, their temples, their couches, the chariot of the sun in his temple-cities, and everything existing in connection with their worship, were in all probability regarded as divine simply in so far as they belonged to a god. Sacrifices offered to them, and invocations made to them, were in all likelihood regarded as having been made to the deity himself, the possessions of the divinity being, in the minds of the Babylonians, pervaded with his spirit. In the case of rivers, these were

---

5 Notwithstanding medical opinion, their phallic origin is doubtful. One is sculptured in the form of an Eastern castellated fortress.

divine as being the children and offspring of Enki[6] (Aa or Êa), the god of the ocean.

The Lord God Enki
Photo: The Jaredite Apostolic Temple

Holy places.

In a country which was originally divided into many small states, each having its own deities, and, to a certain extent, its own religious system, holy places were naturally numerous. As the spot where they placed Paradise, Babylonia was itself a holy place, but in all probability this idea is late, and only came into existence after the legends of the creation and the rise of Merodach to the kingship of heaven had become elaborated into one homogeneous whole.

An interesting list.

One of the most interesting documents referring to the holy places of Babylonia is a tiny tablet found at Nineveh, and preserved in the British

---

6 Enki is the most important deity of the Eberkeit (aka Jaredites) who fled the Tower of Babel and founded a great nation in Mesoamerica. See. *The Sacred Eberkeit Scriptures.*

Museum. This text begins with the word Tiawthu "the sea," and goes on to enumerate, in turn, Tilmun (identified with the island of Bahrein in the Persian Gulf); Engurra (the Abyss, the abode of Enki or Êa), with numerous temples and shrines, including "the holy house," "the temple of the seer of heaven and earth," "the abode of Zer-panîtum," consort of Merodach, "the throne of the holy place," "the temple of the region of Hades," "the supreme temple of life," "the temple of the ear of the corn-deity," with many others, the whole list containing what may be regarded as the chief sanctuaries of the land, to the number of thirty-one. Numerous other similar and more extensive lists, enumerating every shrine and temple in the country, also exist, though in a very imperfect state, and in addition to these, many holy places are referred to in the bilingual, historical, and other inscriptions. All the great cities of Babylonia, moreover, were sacred places, the chief in renown and importance in later days being the great city of Babylon, where Ê-sagila, "the temple of the high head," in which was apparently the shrine called "the temple of the foundation of heaven and earth," held the first place. This building is called by Nebuchadnezzar "the temple-tower of Babylon," and may better be regarded as the site of the Biblical "Tower of Babel" than the traditional foundation, Ê-zida, "the everlasting temple," in Borsippa (the Birs Nimroud)—notwithstanding that Borsippa was called the "second Babylon," and its temple-tower "the supreme house of life."

The Tower of Babel.

Though quite close to Babylon, there is no doubt that Borsippa was a most important religious center, and this leads to the possibility, that its great temple may have disputed with "the house of the high head," Ê-sagila in Babylon, the honor of being the site of the confusion of tongues and the dispersion of mankind. There is no doubt, however, that Ê-sagila has the prior claim, it being the temple of the supreme god of the later Babylonian pantheon, the counterpart of the God of the Hebrews who commanded the changing of the speech of the people assembled there. Supposing the confusion of tongues to have been a Babylonian legend as well as a Hebrew one (as is possible) it would be by command of Merodach rather than that of Nebo that such a thing

15

would have taken place. Ê-sagila, which is now the ruin known as the mount of Amran ibn Ali, is the celebrated temple of Belus which Alexander and Philip attempted to restore.

In addition to the legend of the confusion of tongues, it is probable that there were many similar traditions attached to the great temples of Babylonia, and as time goes on, and the excavations bring more material, a large number of them will probably be recovered. Already we have an interesting and poetical record of the entry of Bel and Beltis into the great temple at Niffer, probably copied from some ancient source, and Gudea, a king of Lagaš (Telloh), who reigned about 2700 B.C., gives an account of the dream which he saw, in which he was instructed by the gods to build or rebuild the temple of Nin-Girsu in his capital city.

Ê-sagila according to Herodotus.

As the chief fane in the land after Babylon became the capital, and the type of many similar erections, Ê-sagila, the temple of Belus, merits just a short notice. According to Herodotus, it was a massive tower within an enclosure measuring 400 yards each way, and provided with gates of brass, or rather bronze. The tower within consisted of a kind of step-pyramid, the stages being seven in number (omitting the lowest, which was the platform forming the foundation of the structure). A winding ascent gave access to the top, where was a chapel or shrine, containing no statue, but regarded by the Babylonians as the abode of the god. Lower down was another shrine, in which was placed a great statue of Zeus (Bel-Merodach) sitting, with a large table before it. Both statue and table are said to have been of gold, as were also the throne and the steps. Outside the sanctuary (on the ramp, apparently) were two altars, one small and made of gold, whereon only unweaned lambs were sacrificed, and the other larger, for full-grown victims.

A Babylonian description.

In 1876 the well-known Assyriologist, Mr. George Smith, was fortunate enough to discover a Babylonian description of this temple, of which he published a /précis/. According to this document, there were two courts of considerable extent, the smaller within the larger—neither of them was square, but oblong. Six gates admitted to the temple-area surrounding the platform upon which the tower was built. The platform is stated to have been square and walled, with four gates facing the cardinal points. Within this wall was a building connected with the great /zikkurat/ or tower—the principal edifice—round which were chapels or temples to the principal gods, on all four sides, and facing the cardinal points—that to Nebo and Tašmît being on the east, to Aa or Êa and Nusku on the north, Anu and Bel on the south, and the series of buildings on the west, consisting of a double house—a small court between two wings, was evidently the shrine of Merodach (Belos). In these western chambers stood the couch of the god, and the golden throne mentioned by Herodotus, besides other furniture of great value. The couch was given as being 9 cubits long by 4 broad, about as many feet in each case, or rather more.

The center of these buildings was the great /zikkurat/, or temple-tower, square on its plan, and with the sides facing the cardinal points. The lowest stage was 15 /gar/ square by 5 1/2 high (Smith, 300 feet by 110), and the wall, in accordance with the usual Babylonian custom, seems to have been ornamented with recessed groovings. The second stage was 13 /gar/ square by 3 in height (Smith, 260 by 60 feet). He conjectured, from the expression used, that it had sloping sides. Stages three to five were each one /gar/ (Smith, 20 feet) high, and respectively 10 /gar/ (Smith, 200 feet), 8 1/2 /gar/ (170 feet), and 7 /gar/ (140 feet) square. The dimensions of the sixth stage are omitted, probably by accident, but Smith conjectures that they were in proportion to those which precede. His description omits also the dimensions of the seventh stage, but he gives those of the sanctuary of Belus, which was built upon it. This was 4 /gar/ long, 3 1/2 /gar/ broad, and 2 1/2 /gar/ high (Smith, 80 x 70 x 50 feet). He points out, that the total height was, therefore, 15 /gar/, the same as the dimensions of the base, i.e., the lowest platform, which would make the total height of this world-renowned building rather more than 300 feet above the plains.

Other temple-towers.

Towers of a similar nature were to be found in all the great cities of Babylonia, and it is probable that in most cases slight differences of form were to be found. That at Niffer, for instance, seems to have had a causeway on each side, making four approaches in the form of a cross. But it was not every city which had a tower of seven stages in addition to the platform on which it was erected, and some of the smaller ones at least seem to have had sloping or rounded sides to the basement-portion, as is indicated by an Assyrian bas-relief. Naturally small temples, with hardly more than the rooms on the ground floor, were to be found, but these temple-towers were a specialty of the country.

Their origin.

There is some probability that, as indicated in the tenth chapter of Genesis, the desire in building these towers was to get nearer the Deity, or to the divine inhabitants of the heavens in general—it would be easier there to gain attention than on the surface of the earth. Then there was the belief, that the god to whom the place was dedicated would come down to such a sanctuary, which thus became, as it were, the stepping-stone between heaven and earth. Sacrifices were also offered at these temple-towers (whether on the highest point or not is not quite certain), in imitation of the Chaldæan Noah, Ut-napištim, who, on coming out of the ark, made an offering /ina zikkurat šadê/, "on the peak of the mountain," in which passage, it is to be noted, the word /zikkurat/ occurs with what is probably a more original meaning.

CHAPTER III

THE BABYLONIAN STORY OF THE CREATION

This is the final development of the Babylonian creed. It has already been pointed out that the religion of the Babylonians in all probability had two stages before arriving at that in which the god Merodach occupied the position of chief of the pantheon, the two preceding heads having been, seemingly, Anu, the god of the heavens, and Êa or Aa, also called Enki, the god of the abyss and of deep wisdom. In order to show this, and at the same time to give an idea of their theory of the beginning of things, a short paraphrase of the contents of the seven tablets will be found in the following pages.

An Embodiment of doctrine.

As far as our knowledge goes, the doctrines incorporated in this legend would seem to show the final official development of the beliefs held by the Babylonians, due, in all probability, to the priests of Babylon after that city became the capital of the federated states. Modifications of their creed probably took place, but nothing seriously affecting it, until after the abandonment of Babylon in the time of Seleucus Nicator, 300 B.C. or thereabouts, when the deity at the head of the pantheon seems not to have been Merodach, but Anu-Bêl. This legend is therefore the most important document bearing upon the beliefs of the Babylonians from the end of the third millennium B.C. until that time, and the philosophical ideas which it contains seem to have been held, in a more or less modified form, among the remnants who still retained the old Babylonian faith, until the sixth century of the present era, as the record by Damascius implies. Properly speaking, it is not a record of the creation, but the story of the fight between Bel and the Dragon, to which the account of the creation is prefixed by way of introduction.

Water the first creator.

he legend begins by stating that, when the heavens were unnamed and the earth bore no name, the primeval ocean was the producer of all things, and Mummu Tiawath (the sea) she who brought forth everything existing. Their waters (that is, of the primeval ocean and of the sea) were all united in one, and neither plains nor marshes were to be seen; the gods likewise did not exist, even in name, and the fates were undetermined—nothing had been decided as to the future of things. Then arose the great gods. Lahmu and Lahame came first, followed, after a long period, by Anšar and Kišar, generally identified with the "host of heaven" and the "host of earth," these being the meanings of the component parts of their names. After a further long period of days, there came forth their son Anu, the god of the heavens.

The gods.

Here the narrative is defective, and is continued by Damascius in his /Doubts and Solutions of the First Principles/, in which he states that, after Anos (Anu), come Illinos (Ellila or Bel, "the lord" /par excellence/) and Aos (Aa, Ae, or Êa), the god of Eridu. Of Aos and Dauké (the Babylonian Aa and Damkina) is born, he says, a son called Belos (Bel-Merodach), who, they (apparently the Babylonians) say, is the fabricator of the world—the creator.

The designs against them.

At this point Damascius ends his extract, and the Babylonian tablet also becomes extremely defective. The next deity to come into existence, however, would seem to have been Nudimmud, who was apparently the deity Aa or Êa (the god of the sea and of rivers) as the god of creation. Among the children of Tauthé (Tiawath) enumerated by Damascius is one named Moumis, who was evidently referred to in the document at that philosopher's disposal. If this be correct, his name, under the form of Mummu, probably existed in one of the defective lines of the first portion of this legend—in any case, his name occurs later on, with those of Tiawath and Apsu (the Deep), his parents, and the three seem to be compared, to their disadvantage, with the progeny of Lahmu and Lahame, the gods on high. As the ways of these last were not those of Tiawath's brood, and Apsu complained that he had no peace by day nor rest by night on account of their proceedings, the three representatives of the chaotic deep, Tiawath, Apsu, and Mummu, discussed how they might get rid the beings who wished to rise to higher things. Mummu was apparently the prime mover in the plot, and the face of Apsu grew bright at the thought of the evil plan which they had devised against "the gods their sons." The inscription being very mutilated here, its full drift cannot be gathered, but from the complete portions which come later it would seem that Mummu's plan was not a remarkably cunning one, being simply to make war upon and destroy the gods of heaven.

Tiawath's preparations.

The preparations made for this were elaborate. Restlessly, day and night, the powers of evil raged and toiled, and assembled for the fight. "Mother Hubur," as Tiawath is named in this passage, called her creative powers into action, and gave her followers irresistible weapons. She brought into being also various monsters—giant serpents, sharp of tooth, bearing stings, and with poison filling their bodies like blood; terrible dragons endowed with brilliance, and of enormous stature, reared on high, raging dogs, scorpion-men, fish-men, and many other terrible beings, were created and equipped, the whole being placed under the command of a deity named Kingu, whom she calls her "only husband," and to whom she delivers the tablets of fate, which conferred upon him the godhead of Anu (the heavens), and enabled their possessor to determine the gates among the gods her sons.

Kingu replaces Absu.

The change in the narrative which comes in here suggests that this is the point at which two legends current in Babylonia were united. Henceforward we hear nothing more of Apsu, the begetter of all things, Tiawath's spouse, nor of Mummu, their son. In all probability there is good reason for this, and inscriptions will doubtless ultimately be found which will explain it, but until then it is only natural to suppose that two different legends have been pieced together to form a harmonious whole.

Tiawath's aim.

As will be gathered from the above, the story centers in the wish of the goddess of the powers of evil and her kindred to retain creation—the forming of all living things—in her own hands. As Tiawath means "the sea," and Apsu "the deep," it is probable that this is a kind of allegory personifying the productive power seen in the teeming life of the ocean, and typifying the strange and wonderful forms found therein, which were symbolical, to the Babylonian mind, of chaos and confusion, as well as of evil.

The gods hear of the conspiracy.

Aa, or Êa, having learned of the plot of Tiawath and her followers against the gods of heaven, naturally became filled with anger, and went and told the whole to Anšar, his father, who in his turn gave way to his wrath, and uttered cries of the deepest grief. After considering what they would do, Anšar applied to his son Anu, "the mighty and brave," saying that, if he would only speak to her, the great dragon's anger would be assuaged, and her rage disappear. In obedience to this behest, Anu went to try his power with the monster, but on beholding her snarling face, feared to approach her, and turned back. Nudimmud was next called upon to become the representative of the gods against their foe, but his success was as that of Anu, and it became needful to seek another champion.

And choose Merodach as their champion.

The choice fell upon Merodach, the Belus (Bel-Merodach) of Damascius's paraphrase, and at once met with an enthusiastic reception. The god asked simply that an "unchangeable command" might be given to him—that whatever he ordained should without fail come to pass, in order that he might destroy the common enemy. Invitations were sent to the gods asking them to a festival, where, having met together, they ate and drank, and "decided the fate" for Merodach their avenger, apparently meaning that he was decreed their defender in the conflict with Tiawath, and that the power of creating and annihilating by the word of his mouth was his. Honors were then conferred upon him; princely chambers were erected for him, wherein he sat as judge "in the presence of his fathers," and the rule over the whole universe was given to him. The testing of his newly acquired power followed. A garment was placed in their midst:

22

"He spake with his mouth, and the garment was destroyed,
He spake to it again, and the garment was reproduced."

Merodach proclaimed king.

On this proof of the reality of the powers conferred on him, all the gods shouted "Merodach is king!" and handed to him scepter, throne, and insignia of royalty. An irresistible weapon, which should shatter all his enemies, was then given to him, and he armed himself also with spear or dart, bow, and quiver; lightning flashed before him, and flaming fire filled his body. Anu, the god of the heavens, had given him a great net, and this he set at the four cardinal points, in order that nothing of the dragon, when he had defeated her, should escape. Seven winds he then created to accompany him, and the great weapon called /Abubu/, "the Flood," completed his equipment. All being ready, he mounted his dreadful, irresistible chariot, to which four steeds were yoked—steeds unsparing, rushing forward, rapid in flight, their teeth full of venom, foam-covered, experienced in galloping, schooled in overthrowing. Being now ready for the fray, Merodach fared forth to meet Tiawath, accompanied by the fervent good wishes of "the gods his fathers."

The fight with Tiawath.

Advancing, he regarded Tiawath's retreat, but the sight of the enemy was so menacing that even the great Merodach (if we understand the text rightly) began to falter. This, however, was not for long, and the king of the gods stood before Tiawath, who, on her side, remained firm and undaunted. In a somewhat long speech, in which he reproaches Tiawath for her rebellion, he challenges her to battle, and the two meet in fiercest fight. To all appearance the type of all evil did not make use of honest weapons, but sought to overcome the king of the gods with incantations and charms. These, however, had not the slightest effect, for she found herself at once enclosed in Merodach's net, and on opening her mouth to resist and free herself, the evil wind, which Merodach had sent on before him, entered, so that she could not close her lips, and thus inflated, her heart was overpowered, and she became a prey to her conqueror. Having cut her asunder and taken out

23

her heart, thus destroying her life, he threw her body down and stood thereon. Her followers then attempted to escape, but found themselves surrounded and unable to get forth. Like their mistress, they were thrown into the net, and sat in bonds, being afterwards shut up in prison. As for Kingu, he was raised up, bound, and delivered to be with Ugga, the god of death. The tablets of fate, which Tiawath had delivered to Kingu, were taken from him by Merodach, who pressed his seal upon them, and placed them in his breast. The deity Anšar, who had been, as it would seem, deprived of his rightful power by Tiawath, received that power again on the death of the common foe, and Nudimmud "saw his desire upon his enemy."

Tiawath's fate.

The dismemberment of Tiawath then followed, and her veins having been cut through, the north wind was caused by the deity to carry her blood away into secret places, a statement which probably typifies the opening of obstructions which prevent the rivers flowing from the north from running into the southern seas, helped thereto by the north wind. Finally her body was divided, like "a /mašdê/-fish," into two parts, one of which was made into a covering for the heavens—the "waters above the firmament" of Genesis i. 7.

Merodach orders the world anew.

Then came the ordering of the universe anew. Having made a covering for the heavens with half the body of the defeated Dragon of Chaos, Merodach set the Abyss, the abode of Nudimmud, in front, and made a corresponding edifice above—the heavens—where he founded stations for the gods Anu, Bel, and Ae. Stations for the great gods in the likeness of constellations, together with what is regarded as the Zodiac, were his next work. He then designated the year, setting three constellations for each month, and made a station for Nibiru—Merodach's own star—as the overseer of all the lights in the firmament. He then caused the new moon, Nannaru, to shine, and made him the ruler of the night, indicating his phases, one of which was on the seventh day, and the other, a /šabattu/, or day of rest, in the middle of the month. Directions with regard to the moon's movements seem to follow, but the record is mutilated, and their real nature consequently doubtful. With regard to other works which were performed we have no information, as a gap prevents their being ascertained. Something, however, seems to have been done with Merodach's net—probably it was placed in the heavens as a constellation, as was his bow, to which several names were given. Later on, the winds were bound and assigned to their places, but the account of the arrangement of other things is mutilated and obscure, though it can be recognized that the details in this place were of considerable interest.

The creation of man.

To all appearance the gods, after he had ordered the universe and the things then existing, urged Merodach to further works of wonder. Taking up their suggestion, he considered what he should do, and then communicated to his father Ae his plan for the creation of man with his own blood, in order that the service and worship of the gods might be established. This portion is also unfortunately very imperfect, and the details of the carrying out of the plan are entirely wanting.

Berosus' narrative fills the gap.

It is noteworthy that this portion of the narrative has been preserved by Abydenus, George the Syncellus, and Eusebius, in their quotations from Berosus. According to this Chaldæan writer, there was a woman named Omoroca, or, in Chaldæan, Thalatth (apparently a mistake for Thauatth, i.e. Tiawath), whose name was equivalent to the Greek Thalassa, the sea. It was she who had in her charge all the strange creatures then existing. At this period, Belus (Bel-Merodach) came, and cut the woman asunder, forming out of one half the earth, and of the other the heavens, at the same time destroying all the creatures which were within her—all this being an allegory, for the whole universe consists of moisture, and creatures are constantly generated therein. The deity then cut off his own head, and the other gods mixed the blood, as it gushed out, with the earth, and from this men were formed. Hence it is that men are rational, and partake of divine knowledge.

A second creation.

This Belsus, "who is called Zeus," divided the darkness, separated the heavens from the earth, and reduced the universe to order. The animals which had been created, however, not being able to bear the light, died. Belus then, seeing the void thus made, ordered one of the gods to take off his head, and mix the blood with the soil, forming other men and animals which should be able to bear the light. He also formed the stars, the sun, the moon, and the five planets. It would thus seem that there were two creations, the first having been a failure because Belus had not foreseen that it was needful to produce beings which should be able to bear the light. Whether this repetition was really in the Babylonian legend, or whether Berosus (or those who quote him) has merely inserted and united two varying accounts, will only be known when the cuneiform text is completed.

The concluding tablet.

The tablet of the fifty-one names completes the record of the tablets found at Nineveh and Babylon. In this Merodach receives the titles of all the other gods, thus identifying him with them, and leading to that tendency to monotheism of which something will be said later on. In this text, which is written, like the rest of the legend, in poetical form, Merodach is repeatedly called /Tutu/, a mystic word meaning "creator," and "begetter," from the reduplicate root /tu/ or /utu/—which was to all appearances his name when it was desired to refer to him especially in that character. Noteworthy in this portion is the reference to Merodach's creation of mankind:—

> Line 25. "Tuto: Aga-azaga (the glorious crown)—may he make the crowns glorious. 26. The lord of the glorious incantation bringing the dead to life; 27. He who had mercy on the gods who had been overpowered; 28. Made heavy the yoke which he had laid on the gods who were his enemies, 29. (And) to redeem(?) them, created mankind. 30. 'The merciful one,' 'he with whom is salvation,' 31. May his word be established, and not forgotten, 32. In the mouth of the black-headed ones (mankind) whom his hands have made."

Man the redeemer.

The phrase "to redeem them" is, in the original, /ana padi-šunu/, the verb being from /padû/, "to spare," "set free," and if this rendering be correct, as seems probable, the Babylonian reasons for the creation of mankind would be, that they might carry on the service and worship of the gods, and by their righteousness redeem those enemies of the gods who were undergoing punishment for their hostility. Whether by this Tiawath, Apsu, Mummu, Kingu, and the monsters whom she had created were included, or only the gods of heaven who had joined her, the record does not say. Naturally, this doctrine depends entirely upon the correctness of the translation of the words quoted. Jensen, who first proposed this rendering, makes no attempt to explain it, and simply asks: "Does 'them' in 'to redeem(?) them' refer to the gods named in line 28 or to mankind and then to a future—how meant?—redemption? Eschatology? Zimmern's 'in their place' unprovable. Delitzsch refrains from an explanation."

The bilingual account of the creation. Aruru aids Merodach.

Whilst dealing with this part of the religious beliefs of the Babylonians, a few words are needed concerning the creation-story which is prefixed to an incantation used in a purification ceremony. The original text is Sumerian (dialectic), and is provided with a Semitic translation. In this inscription, after stating that nothing (in the beginning) existed, and even the great cities and temples of Babylonia were as yet unbuilt, the condition of the world is briefly indicated by the statement that "All the lands were sea." The renowned cities of Babylonia seem to have been regarded as being as much creations of Merodach as the world and its inhabitants—indeed, it is apparently for the glorification of those cities by attributing their origin to Merodach, that the bilingual account of the creation was composed.. "When within the sea there was a stream"—that is, when the veins of Tiawath had been cut through—Êridu (probably = Paradise) and the temple Ê-sagila within the Abyss were constructed, and after that Babylon and the earthly temple of Ê-sagila within it. Then he made the gods and the Annunnaki (the gods of the earth), proclaimed a glorious city as the seat

27

of the joy of their hearts, and afterwards made a pleasant place in which the gods might dwell. The creation of mankind followed, in which Merodach was aided by the goddess Aruru, who made mankind's seed. Finally, plants, trees, and the animals, were produced, after which Merodach constructed bricks, beams, houses, and cities, including Niffer and Erech with their renowned temples.

We see here a change in the teaching with regard to Merodach —the gods are no longer spoken of as "his fathers," but he is the creator of the gods, as well as of mankind.

The order of the gods in the principal lists.

It is unfortunate that no lists of gods have been found in a sufficiently complete state to allow of the scheme after which they were drawn up to be determined without uncertainty. It may, nevertheless, be regarded as probable that these lists, at least in some cases, are arranged in conformity (to a certain extent) with the appearance of the deities in the so-called creation-story. Some of them begin with Anu, and give him various names, among them being Anšar and Kišar, Lahmu and Lahame, etc. More specially interesting, however, is a well-known trilingual list of gods, which contains the names of the various deities in the following order:—

EXTRACTS FROM THE TRILINGUAL LIST
/Obverse/
Sumer. Dialect Sumer. Standard Common Explanation (Semit. or Sumer.)

1. Dimmer Dingir Îlu God. 2. U-ki En-ki Ê-a Êa or Aa. 3. Gašan(?)-ki Nin-ki Dawkina Dauké, the consort of Êa. 4. Mu-ul-lil En-lil-la Bêl The God Bel. 5. E-lum A-lim Bêl 6. Gašan(?)-lil Nin-lil-la dam-bi sal Bel's consort. 7. U-lu-a Ni-rig Ênu-rêštu The god of Niffer. 8. U-lib-a Ni-rig Ênu-rêštu 9-12 have Ênu-rêštu's consort, sister, and attendant. 13. U-šab-sib En-šag-duga Nusku Nusku 14-19 have two other names of Nusku, followed by three names of his consort. A number of names of minor divinities then follow. At line 43 five names of Êa are given, followed by four of Merodach:— 48. U-bi-lu-lu En-bi-lu-lu Marduk Merodach 49. U-Tin-dir

28

ki En-Tin-dir ki Marduk Merodach as "lord of Babylon." 50. U-dimmer-an-kia En-dinger-an-kia Marduk Merodach as "lord god of heaven and earth." 51. U-ab-šar-u En-ab-šar-u Marduk Merodach, apparently as "lord of the 36,000 steers." 52. U-bar-gi-si Nin-bar-gi-si Zer-panîtum Merodach's consort. 53. Gašan-abzu Nin-abzu dam-bi sal "the Lady of the Abyss," his consort.

The remainder of the obverse is mutilated, but gave the names of Nebo in Sumerian, and apparently also of Tašmêtum, his consort. The beginning of the reverse also is mutilated, but seems to have given the names of the sun-god, Šamaš, and his consort, followed by those of Kîttu and Mêšarum, "justice and righteousness," his attendants. Other interesting names are:

/Reverse/

8. U-libir-si En-ubar-si Dumu-zi Tammuz 9. Sir-tumu Sir-du ama Dumuzi-gi the mother of Tammuz 12. Gašan-anna Innanna Ištar Ištar (Venus) as "lady of heaven." 20. Nin-si-anna Innanna mul Ištar the star (the planet Venus). 21. Nin Nin-tag-taga Nanaa a goddess identified with Ištar. 23. U-šah Nina-šah Pap-sukal the gods' messenger. 24. U-banda Lugal-banda Lugal-banda 26. U-Mersi Nin-Girsu Nin-Girsu the chief god of Lagaš. 27. Ma-sib-sib Ga-tum-duga Bau Bau, a goddess identified with Gula.

Four non-Semitic names of Gula follow, of which that in line 31 is the most interesting:—

31. Gašan-ti-dibba Nin-tin-guua Gula "the lady saving from death." 33. Gašan-ki-gal Ereš-ki-gala Allatu Persephone. 36. U-mu-zi-da Nin-giš-zi-da Nin-giš-zida "the lord of the everlasting tree." 37. U-urugal Ne-eri-gal Nerigal Nergal. 42. Mulu-hursag Galu-hursag Amurru the Amorite god. 43. Gašan-gu-edina Nin-gu-edina (apparently the consort of Amurru).

In all probability this list is one of comparatively late date, though its chronological position with regard to the others is wholly uncertain—it may not be later, and may even be earlier, than those beginning with Anu, the god of the heavens. The important thing about it is, that it begins with /ilu/, god, in general, which is written, in the standard dialect (that of the second column) with the same character as that used for the name of Anu. After this comes Aa or Êa, the god of the earth, and his consort, followed by En-lilla, the older Bel—Illinos in Damascius. The name of Êa is repeated again in line 43 and following, where he is apparently re-introduced as the father of Merodach, whose names immediately follow. This peculiarity is also found in other lists of gods and is undoubtedly a reflection of the history of the Babylonian religion. As this list replaces Anu by /îlu/, it indicates the rule of Enki or Êa, followed by that of Merodach, who, as has been shown, became the chief divinity of the Babylonian pantheon in consequence of Babylon having become the capital of the country.

CHAPTER IV

THE PRINCIPAL GODS OF THE BABYLONIANS AND ASSYRIANS

Anu.

The name of this divinity is derived from the Sumero-Akkadian /ana/, "heaven," of which he was the principal deity. He is called the father of the great gods, though, in the creation-story, he seems to be described as the son of Anšar and Kišar. In early names he is described as the father, creator, and god, probably meaning the supreme being. His consort was Anatu, and the pair are regarded in the lists as the same as the Lahmu and Lahame of the creation-story, who, with other deities, are also described as gods of the heavens. Anu was worshiped at Erech, along with Ištar.

Ea.

Is given as if it were the /Semitic/ equivalent of /Enki/, "the lord of the earth," but it would seem to be really a Sumerian word, later written /Ae/, and certain inscriptions suggest that the true reading was /Aa/. His titles are "king of the Abyss, creator of everything, lord of all," the first being seemingly due to the fact that Aa is a word which may, in its reduplicate form, mean "waters," or if read /Êa/, "house of water." He also, like Anu, is called "father of the gods." As this god was likewise "lord of deep wisdom," it was to him that his son Merodach went for advice whenever he was in doubt. On account of his knowledge, he was the god of artisans in general—potters, blacksmiths, sailors, builders, stone-cutters, gardeners, seers, barbers, farmers, etc. This is the Aos (a form which confirms the reading Aa) of Damascius, and the Oannes of the extracts from Berosus, who states that he was "a creature endowed with reason, with a body like that of a fish, and under the fish's head another head, with feet below, like those of a man, with a fish's tail." This description applies fairly well to certain bas-reliefs from Nimroud in the British Museum. The creature described by Berosus lived in the Persian Gulf, landing during the day to teach the inhabitants the building of houses and temples, the cultivation of useful plants, the gathering of fruits, and also geometry, law, and letters. From him, too,

31

came the account of the beginning of things referred to in chapter III. which, in the original Greek, is preceded by a description of the composite monsters said to have existed before Merodach assumed the rule of the universe.

The name of his consort, Damkina or Dawkina, probably means "the eternal spouse," and her other names, /Gašan-ki/ (Sumerian dialectic) and /Nin-ki/ (non-dialectic), "Lady of the earth," sufficiently indicates her province. She is often mentioned in the incantations with Êa.

The forsaking of the worship of Êa /Enki/ as chief god for that of Merodach seems to have caused considerable heartburning in Babylonia, if we may judge from the story of the Flood, for it was on account of his faithfulness that Utnipištim, the Babylonian Noah, attained to salvation from the Flood and immortality afterwards. All through this adventure it was the god Êa who favored him, and afterwards gave him immortality like that of the gods. There is an interesting Sumerian text in which the ship of Êa seems to be described, the woods of which its various parts were formed being named, and in it, apparently, were Enki (Êa), Damgal-nunna (Damkina), his consort, Asari-lu-duga (Merodach), In-ab (or Ineš), the pilot of Êridu (Êa's city), and Nin-igi-nagar-sir, "the great architect of heaven":—

> "May the ship before thee bring fertility,
> May the ship after thee bring joy,
> In thy heart may it make joy of heart . . . ."

Êa was the god of fertility, hence this ending to the poetical description of the ship of Êa.

Bel.

The deity who is mentioned next in order in the list given above is the "older Bel," so called to distinguish him from Bel-Merodach. His principal names were /Mullil/ (dialectic) or /En-lilla/[7] (standard speech),

---

7 Ordinarily pronounced /Illila/, as certain glosses and Damascius's /Illinos/ (for /Illilos/) show.

the /Illinos/ of Damascius. His name is generally translated "lord of mist," so-called as god of the underworld, his consort being /Gašan-lil/ or /Nan-lilla/, "the lady of the mist," in Semitic Babylonian /Bêltu/, "the Lady," par excellence. Bel, whose name means "the lord," was so called because he was regarded as chief of the gods. As there was considerable confusion in consequence of the title Bel having been given to Merodach, Tiglath-pileser I. (about 1200 B.C.) refers to him as the "older Bel" in describing the temple which he built for him at Aššur. Numerous names of men compounded with his occur until the latest times, implying that, though the favorite god was Merodach, the worship of Bel was not forgotten, even at Babylon—that he should have been adored at his own city, Niffur, and at Dur-Kuri-galzu, where Kuri-galzu I. built a temple for "Bel, the lord of the lands," was naturally to be expected. Being, like Êa, a god of the earth, he is regarded as having formed a trinity with Anu, the god of heaven, and Êa, the god of the deep, and prayer to these three was as good as invoking all the gods of the universe. Classification of the gods according to the domain of their power would naturally take place in a religious system in which they were all identified with each other, and this classification indicates, as Jastrow says, a deep knowledge of the powers of nature, and a more than average intelligence among the Babylonians—indeed, he holds it as a proof that, at the period of the older empire, there were schools and students who had devoted themselves to religious speculation upon this point. He also conjectures that the third commandment of the Law of Moses was directed against this doctrine held by the Babylonians.

Beltis.

This goddess was properly only the spouse of the older Bel, but as /Bêltu/, her Babylonian name, simply meant "lady" in general (just as /Bêl/ or /bêlu/ meant "lord"), it became a title which could be given to any goddess, and was in fact borne by Zer-panîtum, Ištar, Nanaa, and others. It was therefore often needful to add the name of the city over which the special /Bêltu/ presided, in order to make clear which of them was meant. Besides being the title of the spouse of the older Bel, having her earthly seat with him in Niffur and other less important shrines, the

33

Assyrians sometimes name Bêltu the spouse of Aššur, their national god, suggesting an identification, in the minds of the priests, with that deity.

Ênu-rêštu or Nirig.[8]

Whether /Ênu-rêštu/ be a translation of /Nirig/ or not, is uncertain, but not improbable, the meaning being "primeval lord," or something similar, and "lord" that of the first element, /ni/, in the Sumerian form. In support of this reading and rendering may be quoted the fact, that one of the descriptions of this divinity is /ašsarid îlani âhê-šu/, "the eldest of the gods his brothers." It is noteworthy that this deity was a special favorite among the Assyrians, many of whose kings, to say nothing of private persons, bore his name as a component part of theirs. In the bilingual poem entitled /Ana-kime gimma/ ("Formed like Anu"), he is described as being the son of Bel (hence his appearance after Bel in the list printed above), and in the likeness of Anu, for which reason, perhaps, his divinity is called "Anuship." Beginning with words praising him, it seems to refer to his attitude towards the gods of hostile lands, against whom, apparently, he rode in a chariot of the sacred lapis-lazuli. Anu having endowed him with terrible glory, the gods of the earth feared to attack him, and his onrush was as that of a storm-flood. By the command of Bel, his course was directed towards Ê-kur, the temple of Bel at Niffur. Here he was met by Nusku, the supreme messenger of Bel, who, with words of respect and of praise, asks him not to disturb the god Bel, his father, in his seat, nor make the gods of the earth tremble in Upšukennaku (the heavenly festival-hall of the gods), and offers him a gift.[9] It will thus be seen that Ênu-rêštu was a rival to the older Bel, whose temple was the great tower in stages called Ê-kura, in which, in all probability, Ê-šu-me-du, the shrine of Ênu-rêštu, was likewise

---

8 /Ênu-rêštu/ is the reading which I have adopted as the Semitic Babylonian equivalent of the name of this divinity, in consequence of the Aramaic transcription given by certain contract-tablets discovered by the American expedition to Niffer, and published by Prof. Clay of Philadelphia.

9 The result of this request is not known, in consequence of the defective state of the tablets.

situated. The inscriptions call him "god of war," though, unlike Nergal, he was not at the same time god of disease and pestilence. To all appearance he was the god of the various kinds of stones, of which another legend states that he "determined their fate." He was "the hero, whose net overthrows the enemy, who summons his army to plunder the hostile land, the royal son who caused his father to bow down to him from afar." "The son who sat not with the nurse, and eschewed(?) the strength of milk," "the offspring who did not know his father." "He rode over the mountains and scattered seed—unanimously the plants proclaimed his name to their dominion, among them like a great wild bull he raises his horns."

Many other interesting descriptions of the deity Nirig (generally read Nin-ip) occur, and show, with those quoted here, that his story was one of more than ordinary interest.

Nusku.

This deity was especially invoked by the Assyrian kings, but was in no wise exclusively Assyrian, as is shown by the fact that his name occurs in many Babylonian inscriptions. He was the great messenger of the gods, and is variously given as "the offspring of the abyss, the creation of Êa," and "the likeness of his father, the first-born of Bel." As Gibil, the fire-god, has likewise the same diverse parentage, it is regarded as likely that these two gods were identical. Nusku was the god whose command is supreme, the counselor of the great gods, the protector of the Igigi (the gods of the heavens), the great and powerful one, the glorious day, the burning one, the founder of cities, the renewer of sanctuaries, the provider of feasts for all the Igigi, without whom no feast took place in Ê-kura. Like Nebo, he bore the glorious specter, and it was said of him that he attacked mightily in battle. Without him the sun-god, the judge, could not give judgment.

All this points to the probability, that Nusku may not have been the fire-god, but the brother of the fire-god, i.e. either flame, or the light of fire. The sun-god, without light, could not see, and therefore could not give judgment: no feast could be prepared without fire and its flame. As the evidence of the presence of the shining orbs in the

heavens—the light of their fires—he was the messenger of the gods, and was honored accordingly. From this idea, too, he became their messenger in general, especially of Bel-Merodach, the younger Bel, whose requests he carried to the god Êa in the Deep. In one inscription he is identified with Nirig or Ênu-rêštu, who is described above.
Merodach.

Concerning this god, and how he arose to the position of king of all the gods of heaven, has been fully shown in chapter III. Though there is but little in his attributes to indicate any connection with Šamaš, there is hardly any doubt that he was originally a sun-god, as is shown by the etymology of his name. The form, as it has been handed down to us, is somewhat shortened, the original pronunciation having been /Amar-uduk/, "the young steer of day," a name which suggests that he was the morning sun. Of the four names given at the end of chapter III., two—"lord of Babylon," and "lord god of heaven and earth,"—may be regarded as expressing his more well-known attributes. /En-ab-šar-u/, however, is a provisional, though not impossible, reading and rendering, and if correct, the "36,000 wild bulls" would be a metaphorical way of speaking of "the 36,000 heroes," probably meaning the gods of heaven in all their grades. The signification of /En-bilulu/ is unknown. Like most of the other gods of the Babylonian pantheon, however, Merodach had many other names, among which may be mentioned /Asari/, which has been compared with the Egyptian Osiris, /Asari-lu-duga/, "/Asari/ who is good," compared with Osiris Unnefer; /Namtila/, "life", /Tutu/, "begetter (of the gods), renewer (of the gods)," /Šar-azaga/, "the glorious incantation," /Mu-azaga/, "the glorious charm," and many others. The last two refer to his being the god who, by his kindness, obtained from his father Êa, dwelling in the abyss, those charms and incantations which benefited mankind, and restored the sick to health. In this connection, a frequent title given to him is "the merciful one," but most merciful was he in that he spared the lives of the gods who, having sided with Taiwath, were his enemies, as is related in the tablet of the fifty-one names. In connection with the fight he bore also the names, "annihilator of the enemy," "rooter out of all evil," "troubler of the evil ones," "life of the whole of the gods." From these names it is clear that Merodach, in defeating Tiawath, annihilated, at the same time, the spirit of evil, Satan, the accuser, of which she was, probably, the Babylonian type. But unlike the Savior in the Christian creed, he saved not only man, at that time uncreated, but the gods of heaven also. As "king of the heavens," he was identified with the largest of the planets, Jupiter, as well as with other heavenly bodies. Traversing the sky in great zigzags, Jupiter seemed to the Babylonians to superintend the stars, and this was regarded as emblematic of Merodach shepherding them—"pasturing the gods like sheep," as the tablet has it.

A long list of gods gives as it were the court of Merodach, held in what was apparently a heavenly /Ê-sagila/, and among the spiritual beings mentioned are /Minâ-îkul-bêli/ and /Minâ-ištî-bêli/, "what my lord has eaten," and "what has my lord drunk," /Nadin-mê-gati/, "he who gives water for the hands," also the two door-keepers, and the four dogs of Merodach, wherein people are inclined to see the four satellites of Jupiter, which, it is thought, were probably visible to certain of the more sharp-sighted stargazers of ancient Babylonia. These dogs were called /Ukkumu/, /Akkulu/, /Ikšsuda/, and /Iltebu/, "Seizer," "Eater," "Grasper," and "Holder." Images of these beings were probably kept in the temple of Ê-sagila at Babylon.

Zer-panîtum.

This was the name of the consort of Merodach, and is generally read Sarp(b)anitum—a transcription which is against the native orthography and etymology, namely, "seed-creatress" (Zer-banîtum). The meaning attributed to this word is partly confirmed by another name which Lehmann has pointed out that she possessed, namely, /Erua/ or /Aru'a/, who, in an inscription of Antiochus Soter (280-260 B.C.) is called "the queen who produces birth," but more especially by the circumstance, that she must be identical with Aruru, who created the seed of mankind along with Merodach. Why she was called "the lady of the abyss," and elsewhere "the voice of the abyss" (/Me-abzu/) is not known. Zer-panîtum was no mere reflection of Merodach, but one of the most important goddesses in the Babylonian pantheon. The tendency of scholars has been to identify her with the moon, Merodach being a solar deity and the meaning "silvery"—/Sarpanitum/, from /sarpu/, one of the words for "silver," was regarded as supporting this idea. She was identified with the Elamite goddess named Elagu, and with the Lahamum of the island of Bahrein, the Babylonian Tilmun.

Nebo and Tašmêtum.

As "the teacher" and "the hearer" these were among the most popular of the deities of Babylonia and Assyria. Nebo (in Semitic Babylonian Nabû) was worshiped at the temple-tower known as Ê-zida, "the ever-lasting house," at Borsippa, now the Birs Nimroud, traditionally regarded as the site of the Tower of Babel, though that title, as has already been shown, would best suit the similar structure known as Ê-sagila, "the house of the high head," in Babylon itself. In composition with men's names, this deity occurs more than any other, even including Merodach himself—a clear indication of the estimation in which the Babylonians and Assyrians held the possession of knowledge. The character with which his name is written means, with the pronunciation of /ak/, "to make," "to create," "to receive," "to proclaim," and with the pronunciation of /me/, "to be wise," "wisdom," "open of ear," "broad of ear," and "to make, of a house," the last probably referring to the design rather than to the actual building. Under the name of /Dim-šara/ he was "the creator of the writing of the scribes," as /Ni-zu/, "the god who knows" (/zu/, "to know"), as /Mermer/, "the speeder(?) of the command of the gods"—on the Sumerian side indicating some connection with Addu or Rimmon, the thunderer, and on the Semitic side with Ênu-rêštu, who was one of the gods' messengers. A small fragment in the British Museum gave his attributes as god of the various cities of Babylonia, but unfortunately their names are lost or incomplete. From what remains, however, we see that Nebo was god of ditching(?), commerce(?), granaries(?), fasting(?), and food; it was he who overthrew the land of the enemy, and who protected planting; and, lastly, he was god of Borsippa.

The worship of Nebo was not always as popular as it became in the later days of the Babylonian empire and after its fall, and Jastrow is of opinion that Hammurabi intentionally ignored this deity, giving the preference to Merodach, though he did not suppress the worship. Why this should have taken place is not by any means certain, for Nebo was a deity adored far and wide, as may be gathered from the fact that there was a mountain bearing his name in Moab, upon which Moses—also an "announcer," adds Jastrow—died. Besides the mountain, there was a city in Moab so named, and another in Judæa. That it was the Babylonian Nebo originally is implied by the form—the Hebrew corresponding word is /nabi/.

How old the worship of Tašmêtum, his consort, is, is doubtful, but her name first occurs in a date of the reign of Hammurabi. Details concerning her attributes are rare, and Jastrow regards this goddess as the result of Babylonian religious speculations. It is noteworthy that her worship appears more especially in later times, but it may be doubted whether it is a product of those late times, especially when we bear in mind the remarkable seal-impression on an early tablet of 3500-4500 B.C., belonging to Lord Amherst of Hackney, in which we see a male figure with wide-open mouth seizing a stag by his horns, and a female figure with no mouth at all, but with very prominent ears, holding a bull in a similar manner. Here we have the "teacher" and the "hearer" personified in a very remarkable manner, and it may well be that this primitive picture shows the idea then prevailing with regard to these two deities. It is to be noted that the name of Tašmêtum has a Sumerian equivalent, namely, /Kurnun/, and that the ideograph by which it is represented is one whose general meaning seems to be "to bind," perhaps with the additional signification of "to accomplish," in which case "she who hears" would also be "she who obeys."

Šamaš and his consort.

At all times the worship of the sun in Babylonia and Assyria was exceedingly popular, as, indeed, was to be expected from his importance as the greatest of the heavenly bodies and the brightest, without whose help men could not live, and it is an exceedingly noteworthy fact that this deity did not become, like Ra in Egypt, the head of the pantheon. This place was reserved for Merodach, also a sun-god, but possessing attributes of a far wider scope. Šamaš is mentioned as early as the reign of Ê-anna-tum, whose date is set at about 4200 B.C., and at this period his Semitic name does not, naturally, occur, the character used being /Utu/, or, in its longer form, /Utuki/.

It is worthy of note that, in consequence of the Babylonian idea of evolution in the creation of the world, less perfect beings brought forth those which were more perfect, and the sun was therefore the offspring of Nannara or Sin, the moon. In accordance with the same idea, the day, with the Semites, began with the evening, the time when the moon became visible, and thus becomes the offspring of the night. In the inscriptions Šamaš is described as "the light of things above and things below, the illuminator of the regions," "the supreme judge of heaven and earth," "the lord of living creatures, the gracious one of the lands." Dawning in the foundation of the sky, he opened the locks and threw wide the gates of the high heavens, and raised his head, covering heaven and earth with his splendor He was the constantly righteous in heaven, the truth within the ears of the lands, the god knowing justice and injustice, righteousness he supported upon his shoulders, unrighteousness he burst asunder like a leather bond, etc. It will thus be seen, that the sun-god was the great god of judgment and justice— indeed, he is constantly alluded to as "the judge," the reason in all probability being, that as the sun shines upon the earth all day long, and his light penetrates everywhere, he was regarded as the god who knew and investigated everything, and was therefore best in a position to judge aright, and deliver a just decision. It is for this reason that his image appears at the head of the stele inscribed with Hammurabi's laws, and legal ceremonies were performed within the precincts of his temples. The chief seats of his worship were the great temples called Ê-babbara, "the house of great light," in the cities of Larsa and Sippar.

he consort of Šamaš was Aa, whose chief seat was at Sippar, side by side with Šamaš. Though only a weak reflex of the sun-god, her worship was exceedingly ancient, being mentioned in an inscription of Man-ištusu, who is regarded as having reigned before Sargon of Agadé. From the fact that, in one of the lists, she has names formed by reduplicating the name of the sun-god, /Utu/, she would seem once to have been identical with him, in which case it may be supposed that she personified the setting sun—"the double sun" from the magnified disc which he presents at sunset, when, according to a hymn to the setting sun sung at the temple at Borsippa, Aa, in the Sumerian line Kur-nirda, was accustomed to go to receive him. According to the list referred to above, Aa, with the name of Burida in Sumerian, was more especially the consort of Ša-zu, "him who knows the heart," one of the names of Merodach, who was probably the morning sun, and therefore the exact counterpart of the sun at evening.

Besides Šamaš and Utu, the latter his ordinary Sumerian name, the sun-god had several other non-Semitic names, including /Gišnu/,[10] "the light," /Ma-banda-anna/, "the bark of heaven," /U-ê/, "the rising sun," /Mitra/, apparently the Persian Mithra; /Ume-šimaš/ and Nahunda, Elamite names, and Sahi, the Kassite name of the sun. He also sometimes bears the names of his attendants Kittu and Mêšaru, "Truth" and "Righteousness," who guided him upon his path as judge of the earth.

Tammuz and Ištar.

The date of the rise of the myth of Tammuz is uncertain, but as the name of this god is found on tablets of the time of Lugal-anda and Uru-ka-gina (about 3500 B.C.), it can hardly be of later date than 4000 B.C., and may be much earlier. As he is repeatedly called "the shepherd," and had a domain where he pastured his flock, Professor Sayce sees in Tammuz "Daonus or Daos, the shepherd of Pantibibla," who, according to Berosus, ruled in Babylonia for 10 /sari/, or 36,000 years, and was the sixth king of the mythical period. According to the classic story, the mother of Tammuz had unnatural intercourse with her own father, being urged thereto by Aphrodite whom she had offended, and who had decided thus to avenge herself. Being pursued by her father, who wished to kill her for this crime, she prayed to the gods, and was turned into a tree, from whose trunk Adonis was afterwards born. Aphrodite was so charmed with the infant that, placing him in a chest, she gave him into the care of Persephone, who, however, when she discovered what a treasure she had in her keeping, refused to part with him again. Zeus was appealed to, and decided that for four months in the year Adonis should be left to himself, four should be spent with Aphrodite,

---

10 It is the group expressing this word which is used for Šamaš in the name of Šamaš-šum-ukîn (Saosduchinos), the brother of Aššur-bani-âpli (Assurbanipal). The Greek equivalent implies the pronunciation /Šawaš/, as well as /Šamaš/.

41

and four with Persephone, and six with Aphrodite on earth. He was afterwards slain, whilst hunting, by a wild boar.

Nothing has come down to us as yet concerning this legend except the incident of his dwelling in Hades, whither Ištar, the Babylonian Venus, went in search of him. It is not by any means unlikely, however, that the whole story existed in Babylonia, and thence spread to Phœnicia, and afterwards to Greece. In Phœnicia it was adapted to the physical conditions of the country, and the place of Tammuz's encounter with the boar was said to be the mountains of Lebanon, whilst the river named after him, Adonis (now the Nahr Ibrahim), which ran red with the earth washed down by the autumn rains, was said to be so colored in consequence of being mingled with his blood. The descent of Tammuz to the underworld, typified by the flowing down of the earth-laden waters of the rivers to the sea, was not only celebrated by the Phœnicians, but also by the Babylonians, who had at least two series of lamentations which were used on this occasion, and were probably the originals of those chanted by the Hebrew women in the time of Ezekiel (about 597 B.C.). Whilst on earth, he was the one who nourished the ewe and her lamb, the goat and her kid, and also caused them to be slain—probably in sacrifice. "He has gone, he has gone to the bosom of the earth," the mourners cried, "he will make plenty to overflow for the land of the dead, for its lamentations for the day of his fall, in the unpropitious month of his year." There was also lamentation for the cessation of the growth of vegetation, and one of these hymns, after addressing him as the shepherd and husband of Ištar, "lord of the underworld," and "lord of the shepherd's seat," goes on to liken him to a germ which has not absorbed water in the furrow, whose bud has not blossomed in the meadow; to the sapling which has not been planted by the watercourse, and to the sapling whose root has been removed. In the "Lamentations" in the Manchester Museum, Ištar, or one of her devotees, seems to call for Tammuz, saying, "Return, my husband," as she makes her way to the region of gloom in quest of him. Ereš-ê-gala, "the lady of the great house" (Persephone), is also referred to, and the text seems to imply that Ištar entered her domain in spite of her. In this text other names are given to him, namely, /Tumu-giba/, "son of the flute," /Ama-elaggi/, and /Ši-umunnagi/, "life of the people."

The reference to sheep and goats in the British Museum fragment recalls the fact that in an incantation for purification the person using it is told to get the milk of a yellow goat which has been brought forth in the sheep-fold of Tammuz, recalling the flocks of the Greek sun-god Helios. These were the clouds illuminated by the sun, which were likened to sheep—indeed, one of the early Sumerian expressions for "fleece" was "sheep of the sky." The name of Tammuz in Sumerian is Dumu-zi, or in its rare fullest form, Dumu-zida, meaning "true" or "faithful son." There is probably some legend attached to this which is at present unknown.

In all probability Ištar, the spouse of Tammuz, is best known from her descent into Hades in quest of him when with Persephone (Ereš-ki-gal) in the underworld. In this she had to pass through seven gates, and an article of clothing was taken from her at each, until she arrived in the underworld quite naked, typifying the teaching, that man can take nothing away with him when he departs this life. During her absence, things naturally began to go wrong upon the earth, and the gods were obliged to intervene, and demand her release, which was ultimately granted, and at each gate, as she returned, the adornments which she had left were given back to her. It is uncertain whether the husband whom she sought to release was set free, but the end of the inscription seems to imply that Ištar was successful in her mission.

In this story she typifies the faithful wife, but other legends show another side of her character, as in that of Gilgameš, ruler of her city Erech, to whom she makes love. Gilgameš, however, knowing the character of the divine queen of his city too well, reproaches her with her treatment of her husband and her other lovers—Tammuz, to whom, from year to year, she caused bitter weeping; the bright colored Allala bird, whom she smote and broke his wings; the lion perfect in strength, in whom she cut wounds "by sevens"; the horse glorious in war, to whom she caused hardship and distress, and to his mother Silili bitter weeping; the shepherd who provided for her things which she liked, whom she smote and changed to a jackal; Išullanu, her father's gardener, whom she tried, apparently, to poison, but failing, she smote him, and changed him to a statue(?). On being thus reminded of her misdeeds, Ištar was naturally angry, and, ascending to heaven, complained to her father Anu and her mother Anatu, the result being, that a divine bull was sent against Gilgameš and Enki-du, his friend and helper. The bull, however, was killed, and a portion of the animal having been cut off, Enki-du threw it at the goddess, saying at the same time that, if he could only get hold of her, he would treat her similarly. Apparently Ištar recognized that there was nothing further to be done in the matter, so, gathering the hand-maidens, pleasure-women and whores, in their presence she wept over the portion of the divine bull which had been thrown at her.

The worship of Ištar, she being the goddess of love and war, was considerably more popular than that of her spouse, Tammuz, who, as among the western Semitic nations, was adored rather by the women than the men. Her worship was in all probability of equal antiquity, and branched out, so to say, in several directions, as may be judged by her many names, each of which had a tendency to become a distinct personality. Thus the syllabaries give the character which represents her name as having also been pronounced /Innanna/, /Ennen/, and /Nin/, whilst a not uncommon name in other inscriptions is /Ama-Innanna/, "mother Ištar." The principal seat of her worship in Babylonia was at Erech, and in Assyria at Nineveh—also at Arbela, and many other places. She was also honored (at Erech and elsewhere) under the Elamite names of Tišpak and Šušinak, "the Susian goddess."

Nina.

From the name /Nin/, which Ištar bore, there is hardly any doubt that she acquired the identification with Nina, which is provable as early as the time of the Lagašite kings, Lugal-anda and Uru-ka-gina. As identified with Aruru, the goddess who helped Merodach to create mankind, Ištar was also regarded as the mother of all, and in the Babylonian story of the Flood, she is made to say that she had begotten man, but like "the sons of the fishes," he filled the sea. Nina, then, as another form of Ištar, was a goddess of creation, typified in the teeming life of the ocean, and her name is written with a character standing for a house or receptacle, with the sign for "fish" within. Her earliest seat was the city of Nina in southern Babylonia, from which place, in all probability, colonists went northwards, and founded another shrine at Nineveh in Assyria, which afterwards became the great center of her worship, and on this account the city was called after her Ninaa or Ninua. As their tutelary goddess, the fishermen in the neighborhood of the Babylonian Nina and Lagaš were accustomed to make to her, as well as to Innanna or Ištar, large offerings of fish.

As the masculine deities had feminine forms, so it is not by any means improbable that the goddesses had masculine forms, and if that be the case, we may suppose that it was a masculine counterpart of Nina who founded Nineveh, which, as is well known, is attributed to Ninos, the same name as Nina with the Greek masculine termination.

Nin-Gursu.

This deity is principally of importance in connection with the ancient Babylonian state of Lagaš, the home of an old and important line of kings and viceroys, among the latter being the celebrated Gudea, whose statues and inscribed cylinders now adorn the Babylonian galleries of the Louvre at Paris. His name means "Lord of Girsu," which was probably one of the suburbs, and the oldest part, of Lagaš. This deity was son of En-lila or Bêl, and was identified with Nirig or Ênu-rêštu. To all appearance he was a sun-deity. The dialectic form of his name was /U-Mersi/, of which a variant, /En-Mersi/, occurs in an incantation published in the fourth volume of the /Cuneiform Inscriptions of Western Asia/, pl. 27, where, for the Sumerian "Take a white kid of En-Mersi," the Semitic translation is "of Tammuz," showing that he was identified with the latter god. In the second volume of the same work Nin-Girsu is given as the pronunciation of the name of the god of agriculturalists, confirming this identification, Tammuz being also god of agriculture.

Bau.

This goddess at all times played a prominent part in ancient Babylonian religion, especially with the rulers before the dynasty of Hammurabi. She was the "mother" of Lagaš, and her temple was at Uru-azaga, a district of Lagaš, the chief city of Nin Girsu, whose spouse she

45

was. Like Nin-Girsu, she planted (not only grain and vegetation, but also the seed of men). In her character of the goddess who gave life to men, and healed their bodies in sickness, she was identified with Gula, one of those titles is "the lady saving from death". Ga-tum-duga, whose name probably means "making and producing good," was also exceedingly popular in ancient times, and though identified with Bau, is regarded by Jastrow has having been originally distinct from her.

Ereš-ki-gal or Allatu.

As the prototype of Persephone, this goddess is one of much importance for comparative mythology, and there is a legend concerning her of considerable interest. The text is one of those found at Tel-el-Armana, in Egypt, and states that the gods once made a feast, and sent to Ereš-ki-gal, saying that, though they could go down to her, she could not ascend to them, and asking her to send a messenger to fetch away the food destined for her. This she did, and all the gods stood up to receive her messenger, except one, who seems to have withheld this token of respect. The messenger, when he returned, apparently related to Ereš-ki-gal what had happened, and angered thereat, she sent him back to the presence of the gods, asking for the delinquent to be delivered to her, that she might kill him. The gods then discussed the question of death with the messenger, and told him to take to his mistress the god who had not stood up in his presence. When the gods were brought together, that the culprit might be recognized, one of them remained in the background, and on the messenger asking who it was who did not stand up, it was found to be Nerigal. This god was duly sent, but was not at all inclined to be submissive, for instead of killing him, as she had threatened, Ereš-ki-gal found herself seized by the hair and dragged from her throne, whilst the death-dealing god made ready to cut off her head. "Do not kill me, my brother, let me speak to thee," she cried, and on his loosing his hold upon her hair, she continued, "thou shalt be my husband, and I will be thy wife—I will cause you to take dominion in the wide earth. I will place the tablet of wisdom in thine hand—thou shalt be lord, I will be lady." Nerigal thereupon took her, kissed her, and wiped away her tears, saying, "Whatever thou hast asked me for months past now receives assent."

Ereš-ki-gal did not treat her rival in the affections of Tammuz so gently when Ištar descended to Hades in search of the "husband of her youth." According to the story, not only was Ištar deprived of her garments and ornaments, but by the orders of Ereš-ki-gal, Namtar smote her with disease in all her members. It was not until the gods intervened that Ištar was set free. The meaning of her name is "lady of the great region," a description which is supposed to apply to Hades, and of which a variant, Ereš-ki-gal, "lady of the great house," occurs in the Hymns to Tammuz in the Manchester Museum.

Nergal.

This name is supposed to mean "lord of the great habitation," which would be a parallel to that of his spouse Ereš-ki-gal. He was the ruler of Hades, and at the same time god of war and of disease and pestilence. As warrior, he naturally fought on the side of those who worshiped him, as in the phrase which describes him as "the warrior, the fierce storm-flood overthrowing the land of the enemy." As pointed out by Jastrow, he differs from Nirig, who was also a god of war, in that he symbolizes, as god of disease and death, the misery and destruction which accompany the strife of nations. It is in consequence of this side of his character that he appears also as god of fire, the destroying element, and Jensen says that Nerigal was god of the midday or of the summer sun, and therefore of all the misfortunes caused by an excess of his heat.

The chief center of his worship was Cuthah (/Kutû/, Sumerian /Gudua/) near Babylon, now represented by the mounds of Tel Ibrahim. The identity with the Greek Aries and the Roman Mars is proved by the fact that his planet was /Muštabarrû-mûtanu/, "the death-spreader," which is probably the name of Mars in Semitic Babylonian.

Amurru.

Although this is not by any means a frequent name among the deities worshiped in Babylonia, it is worthy of notice on account of its

47

bearing upon the date of the compilation of the tablet which has been taken as a basis of this list of gods. He was known as "Lord of the mountains," and his worship became very popular during the period of the dynasty to which Hammurabi belonged—say from 2200 to 1937 B.C., when Amurru was much combined with the names of men, and is found both on tablets and cylinder-seals. The ideographic manner of writing it is /Mar-tu/, a word that is used for /Amurru/, the land of the Amorites, which stood for the West in general. Amorites had entered Babylonia in considerable numbers during this period, so that there is but little doubt that his popularity was largely due to their influence, and the tablet containing these names was probably drawn up, or at least had the Semitic equivalents added, towards the beginning of that period.

Sin or Nannara.

The cult of the moon-god was one of the most popular in Babylonia, the chief seat of his worship being at Uru (now Muqayyar) the Biblical Ur of the Chaldees. The origin of the name Sin is unknown, but it is thought that it may be a corruption of Zu-ena, "knowledge-lord," as the compound ideograph expressing his name may be read and translated. Besides this compound ideograph, the name of the god Sin was also expressed by the character for "30," provided with the prefix of divinity, an ideograph which is due to the thirty days of the month, and is thought to be of late date. With regard to Nannar, Jastrow explains it as being for Narnar, and renders it "light-producer." In a long hymn to this god he is described in many lines as "the lord, prince of the gods, who in heaven alone is supreme," and as "father Nannar." Among his other descriptive titles are "great Anu" (Sum. /ana gale/, Semitic Bab. /Anu rabû/)—another instance of the identification of two deities. He was also "lord of Ur," "lord of the temple Gišnu-gala," "lord of the shining crown," etc. He is also said to be "the mighty steer whose horns are strong, whose limbs are perfect, who is bearded with a beard of lapis-stone,[11] who is filled with beauty and fullness (of splendor)."

Besides Babylonia and Assyria, he was also worshiped in other

---

11 Probably of the color of lapis only, not made of the stone itself.

parts of the Semitic east, especially at Harran, to which city Abraham migrated, scholars say, in consequence of the patron-deity being the same as at Ur of the Chaldees, where he had passed the earlier years of his life. The Mountain of Sinai and the Desert of Sin, both bear his name. According to king Dungi (about 2700 B.C.), the spouse of Sin or Nannara was Nin-Uruwa, "the lady of Ur." Sargon of Assyria (722-705 B.C.) calls her Nin-gala.

Addu or Rammanu.

The numerous names which Hadad bears in the inscriptions, both non-Semitic and Semitic, testify to the popularity which this god enjoyed at all times in Babylonia. Among his non-Semitic names may be mentioned Mer, Mermer, Muru, all, it may be imagined, imitative. Addu is explained as being his name in the Amorite language, and a variant form, apparently, which has lost its first syllable, namely, Dadu, also appears—the Assyrians seem always to have used the terminationless form of Addu, namely, Adad. In all probability Addu, Adad, and Dadu are derived from the West Semitic Hadad, but the other name, Rammanu, is native Babylonian, and cognate with Rimmon, which is thus shown by the Babylonian form to mean "the thunderer," or something similar. He was the god of winds, storms, and rain, feared on account of the former, and worshiped, and his favor sought, on account of the last. In his name Birqu, he appears as the god of lightning, and Jastrow is of opinion, that he is sometimes associated on that account with Šamaš, both of them being (although in different degrees) gods of light, and this is confirmed by the fact that, in common with the sun-god, he was called "god of justice." In the Assyrian inscriptions he appears as a god of war, and the kings constantly compare the destruction which their armies had wrought with that of "Adad the inundator." For them he was "the mighty one, inundating the regions of the enemy, lands and houses," and was prayed to strike the land of the person who showed hostility to the Assyrian king, with evil-working lightning, to throw want, famine, drought, and corpses therein, to order that he should not live one day longer, and to destroy his name and his seed in the land.

The original seat of his worship was Muru in South Babylonia, to

49

which the patesi of Girsu in the time of Ibi-Sin sent grain as an offering. Its site is unknown. Other places (or are they other names of the same?) where he was worshiped were Ennigi and Kakru. The consort of Addu was Šala, whose worship was likewise very popular, and to whom there were temples, not only in Babylonia and Assyria, but also in Elam, seemingly always in connection with Addu.

Aššur.

In all the deities treated of above, we see the chief gods of the Babylonian and Assyrian pantheon, which were worshiped by both peoples extensively, none of them being specifically Assyrian, though worshiped by the Assyrians. There was one deity, however, whose name will not be found in the Babylonian lists of gods, namely, Aššur, the national god of Assyria, who was worshiped in the city of Aššur, the old capital of the country.

From this circumstance, it may be regarded as certain, that Aššur was the local god of the city whose name he bore, and that he attained to the position of chief god of the Assyrian pantheon in the same way as Merodach became king of the gods in Babylonia—namely, because Aššur was the capital of the country. His acceptance as chief divinity, however, was much more general than that of Merodach, as temples to him were to be found all over the Assyrian kingdom—a circumstance which was probably due to Assyria being more closely united in itself than Babylonia, causing his name to arouse patriotic feelings wherever it might be referred to. This was probably partly due to the fact, that the king in Assyria was more the representative of the god than in Babylonia, and that the god followed him on warlike expeditions, and when engaged in religious ceremonies—indeed, it is not by any means improbable that he was thought to follow him wherever he went. On the sculptures he is seen accompanying him in the form of a circle provided with wings, in which is shown sometimes a full-length figure of the god in human form, sometimes the upper part only, facing towards and drawing his bow against the foe. In consequence of its general appearance, the image of the god has been likened to the sun in eclipse, the far-stretching wings being thought to resemble the long streamers visible at the moment of totality, and it must be admitted as probable that this may have given the idea of the symbol shown on the sculptures. As a sun-god, and at the same time not the god Šamaš, he resembled the Babylonian Merodach, and was possibly identified with him, especially as, in at least one text, Bêltu (Bêltis) is described as his consort, which would possibly identify Aššur's spouse with Zer-panîtum. The original form of his name would seem to have been Aušar, "water-field," probably from the tract where the city of Aššur was built. His identification with Merodach, if that was ever accepted, may have been due to the likeness of the word to Asari, one of that deity's names. The pronunciation Aššur, however, seems to have led to a comparison with the Anšar of the first tablet of the Creation-story, though it may seem strange that the Assyrians should have thought that their patron-god was a deity symbolizing the "host of heaven." Nevertheless, the Greek transcription of Anšar, namely, /Assoros/, given by Damascius, certainly strengthens the indications of the ideograph in this matter. Delitzsch regards the word Aššur, or Ašur, as he reads it, as meaning "holy," and quotes a list of the gods of the city of Nineveh, where the word Aššur occurs three times, suggesting the exclamation "holy, holy, holy," or "the holy, holy, holy one." In all probability, however, the repetition of the name three times simply means that there were three temples dedicated to Aššur in the cities in question.[12] Jastrow agrees with Delitzsch in regarding Ašur as another form of Ašir (found in early Cappadocian names), but he translates it rather as "overseer" or "guardian" of the land and the people—the terminationless form of /aširu/, which has this meaning, and is applied to Merodach.

As the use of the characters /An-šar/ for the god Aššur only appears at a late date (Jastrow says the eighth century B.C.), this would seem to have been the work of the scribes, who wished to read into the name the earlier signification of Anšar, "the host of heaven," an explanation fully in accord with Jastrow's reasonings with regard to the nature of the deity. As he represented no personification or power of

---

12   Or there may have been three shrines to Aššur in each temple referred to.

nature, he says, but the general protecting spirit of the land, the king, the army, and the people, the capital of the country could be transferred from Aššur to Calah, from there back to Aššur, and finally to Nineveh, without affecting the position of the protecting god of the land in any way. He needed no temple—though such things were erected to him— he had no need to fear that he should suffer in esteem by the preference for some other god. As the embodiment of the spirit of the Assyrian people the personal side of his being remained to a certain extent in the background. If he was the "host of heaven," all the deities might be regarded as having their being in him.

Such was the chief deity of the Assyrians—a national god, grafted on to, but always distinct from, the rest of the pantheon, which, as has been shown, was of Babylonian origin, and always maintained the characteristics and stamp of its origin.

The spouse of Aššur does not appear in the historical texts, and her mention elsewhere under the title of Bêltu, "the lady," does not allow of any identification being made. In one inscription, however, Aššuritu is called the goddess, and Aššur the god, of the star Sib-zi-anna, identified by Jensen with Regulus, which was apparently the star of Merodach in Babylonia. This, however, brings us no nearer, for Aššuritu would simply mean "the Assurite (goddess)."

The minor divinities.

Among the hundreds of names which the lists furnish, a few are worthy of mention, either because of more than ordinary interest, or in consequence of their furnishing the name of some deity, chief in its locality, but identified elsewhere with one of the greater gods.

Aa.—This may be regarded either as the god Êa (though the name is written differently), or as the sun-god assuming the name of his consort; or (what is, perhaps, more probable) as a way of writing A'u or Ya'u (the Hebrew Jah), without the ending of the nominative. This last is also found under the form /Aa'u/, /ya'u/, /yau/, and /ya/.

Abil-addu.—This deity seems to have attained a certain popularity   in later times, especially among immigrants from the West. As "the son of Hadad," he was the equivalent of the Syrian Ben-Hadad. A tablet in New York shows that his name was weakened in form to /Ablada/.

Aku, the moon-god among the heavenly bodies. It is this name which is regarded as occurring in the name of the Babylonian king Eri-Aku, "servant of the moon-god," the biblical Arioch (Gen. xiv.).

Amma-an-ki, Êa or Aa as lord of heaven and earth.

Amna.—A name only found in a syllabary, and assigned to the sun-god, from which it would seem that it is a form of the Egyptian Ammon.

Anunitum, the goddess of one of the two Sippars, called Sippar of Anunitum, who was worshiped in the temple Ê-ulmaš within the city of Agadé (Akkad). Sayce identifies, on this account, these two places as being the same. In a list of stars, Anunitum is coupled with Šinunutum, which are explained as (the stars of) the Tigris and Euphrates. These were probably names of Venus as the morning and evening (or evening and morning) star.

Apsu.—The deep dissociated from the evil connection with Tiawath, and regarded as "the house of deep wisdom," i.e. the home of the god Êa or Aa.

Aruru.—One of the deities of Sippar and Aruru (in the time of the dynasty of Hammurabi called Ya'ruru), of which she was the chief goddess. Aruru was one of the names of the "lady of the gods," and aided Merodach to make the seed of mankind.

Bêl.—As this name means "lord," it could be applied, like the Phœnician Baal, to the chief god of any city, as Bêl of Niffur, Bêl of Hursag-kalama, Bêl of Aratta, Bêl of Babylon, etc. This often indicates also the star which represented the chief god of a place.

Bêltu.—In the same way Bêltu, meaning "lady," meant also the chief goddess of any place, as "Aruru, lady of the gods of Sippar of Aruru," "Nin-mah, lady of the gods of Ê-mah," a celebrated temple within Babylon, recently excavated by the Germans, "Nin-hur-saga, lady of the gods of Kêš," etc.

Bunene.—A god associated with Šamaš and Ištar at Sippar and elsewhere. He "gave" and "renewed" to his worshipers

Dagan.—This deity, whose worship extends back to an

exceedingly early date, is generally identified with the Phœnician Dagon. Hammurabi seems to speak of the Euphrates as being "the boundary of Dagan," whom he calls his creator. In later inscriptions the form Daguna, which approaches nearer to the West Semitic form, is found in a few personal names. The Phœnician statues of this deity showed him with the lower part of his body in the form of a fish (see 1 Sam. v. 4). Whether the deities clothed in a fish's skin in the Nimroud gallery be Dagon or not is uncertain—they may be intended for Êa or Aa, the Oannes of Berosus, who was represented in this way. Probably the two deities were regarded as identical.

Damu.—a goddess regarded as equivalent to Gula by the Babylonians and Assyrians. She was goddess of healing, and made one's dreams happy.

Dumu-zi-abzu, "Tammuz of the Abyss."—This was one of the six sons of Êa or Aa, according to the lists. His worship is exceedingly ancient, and goes back to the time of E-anna-tum of Lagaš (about 4000 B.C.). What connection, if any, he may have with Tammuz, the spouse of Ištar, is unknown. Jastrow apparently regards him as a distinct deity, and translates his name "the child of the life of the water-deep."

Elali.—A deity identified with the Hebrew Helal, the new moon. Only found in names of the time of the Hammurabi dynasty, in one of which he appears as "a creator."

En-nugi is described as "lord of streams and canals," and "lord of the earth, lord of no-return." This last description, which gives the meaning of his name, suggests that he was one of the gods of the realm of Ereš-ki-gal, though he may have borne that name simply as god of streams, which always flow down, never the reverse.

Gibil.—One of the names of the god of fire, sometimes transcribed Girru by Assyriologists, the meaning apparently being "the fire-bearer" or "light-bearer." Girru is another name of this deity, and translates an ideographic group, rendered by Delitzsch "great" or "highest decider," suggesting the custom of trial by ordeal. He was identified with Nirig, in Semitic Ênu-rêštu.

Gušqi-banda or Kuski-banda, one of the names of Êa, probably as god of gold-workers.

Išum, "the glorious sacrificer," seemingly a name of the fire-god as a means whereby burnt offerings were made. Nûr-Išum, "light of Išum," is found as a man's name.

Kâawanu, the planet Saturn.

Lagamal.—A god identified with the Elamite Lagamar, whose name is regarded as existing in Chedorlaomer (cf. Gen. xiv. 2). He was the chief god of Mair, "the ship-city."

Lugal-Amarada or Lugal-Marad.—This name means "king of Marad," a city as yet unidentified. The king of this place seems to have been Nerigal, of whom, therefore, Lugal-Marad is another name.

Lugal-banda.—This name means "the powerful king," or something similar, and the god bearing it is supposed to be the same as Nerigal. His consort, however, was named Nin-sun (or Nin-gul).

Lugal-Du-azaga, "the king of the glorious seat."—The founder of Êridu, "the good city within the Abyss," probably the paradise (or a paradise) of the world to come. As it was the aim of every good Babylonian to dwell hereafter with the god whom he had worshiped upon earth, it may be conjectured that this was the paradise in the domain of Êa or Aa.

Mama, Mami.—Names of "the lady of the gods," and creatress of the seed of mankind, Aruru. Probably so called as the "mother" of all things. Another name of this goddess is Ama, "mother."

Mammitum, Mamitum, goddess of fate.

Mur, one of the names of Addu or Rammanu (Hadad or Rimmon).

Nanâ or Nanaa was the consort of Nebo at Borsippa, but appears as a form of Ištar, worshiped, with Anu her father, at Erech.

Nin-aha-kuku, a name of Êa or Aa and of his daughter as deity of the rivers, and therefore of gardens and plantations, which were watered by means of the small canals leading therefrom. As daughter of Êa, this deity was also "lady of the incantation."

Nin-azu, the consort of Ereš-ki-gal, probably as "lord physician." He is probably to be identified with Nerigal.

Nin-igi-nagar-si, a name somewhat more doubtful as to its reading than the others, designates Êa or Aa as "the god of the carpenter." He seems to have borne this as "the great constructor of heaven" or "of Anu."

Nin-mah, chief goddess of the temple Ê-mah in Babylon.

Probably to be identified with Aruru, and therefore with Zer-panîtum.

Nin-šah, a deity whose name is conjectured to mean "lord of the wild boar." He seems to have been a god of war, and was identified with Nirig or Ênu-rêštu and Pap-sukal.

Nin-sirsir, Êa as the god of sailors.

Nin-sun, as pointed out by Jastrow, was probably the same as Ištar or Nanâ of Erech, where she had a shrine, with them, in Ê-anna, "the house of Anu." He renders her name "the annihilating lady,"[13] "appropriate for the consort of a sun-god," for such he regards Lugal-banda her spouse. King Sin-gasid of Erech (about 3000 B.C.) refers to her as his mother.

Nun-urra.—Êa, as the god of potters.

Pap-sukal.—A name of Nin-šah as the "divine messenger," who is also described as god "of decisions." Nin-šah would seem to have been one of the names of Pap-sukal rather than the reverse.

Qarradu, "strong," "mighty," "brave."—This word, which was formerly translated "warrior," is applied to several deities, among them being Bêl, Nergal, Nirig (Ênu-rêštu), and Šamaš, the sun-god.

Ragimu and Ramimu, names of Rimmon or Hadad as "the thunderer." The second comes from the same root as Rammanu (Rimmon).

Šuqamunu.—A deity regarded as "lord of watercourses," probably the artificial channels dug for the irrigation of fields.

Ura-gala, a name of Nerigal.

Uraš, a name of Nirig, under which he was worshiped at Dailem, near Babylon.

Zagaga, dialectic Zamama.—This deity, who was a god of war, was identified with Nirig. One of this titles was /bêl parakki/, "lord of the royal chamber," or "throne-room."

Zaraqu or Zariqu.—As the root of this name means "to sprinkle," he was probably also a god of irrigation, and may have presided over ceremonial purification. He is mentioned in names as the "giver of seed" and "giver of a name" (i.e. offspring).

---

13 This is due to the second element of the name having, with another pronunciation, the meaning of "to destroy."

These are only a small proportion of the names found in the inscriptions, but short as the list necessarily is, the nature, if not the full composition, of the Babylonian pantheon will easily be estimated therefrom.

It will be seen that besides the identifications of the deities of all the local pantheons with each other, each divinity had almost as many names as attributes and titles, hence their exceeding multiplicity. In such an extensive pantheon, many of the gods composing it necessarily overlap, and identification of each other, to which the faith, in its primitive form, was a stranger, were inevitable. The tendency to monotheism which this caused will be referred to later on.

The gods and the heavenly bodies.

It has already been pointed out that, from the evidence of the Babylonian syllabary, the deities of the Babylonians were not astral in their origin, the only gods certainly originating in heavenly bodies being the sun and the moon. This leads to the supposition that the Babylonians, bearing these two deities in mind, may have asked themselves why, if these two were represented by heavenly bodies, the others should not be so represented also. Be this as it may, the other deities of the pantheon were so represented, and the full planetary scheme, as given by a bilingual list in the British Museum, was as follows:

Aku Sin the moon Sin
Bišebi Šamaš the sun Šamaš
Dapinu Umun-sig-êa Jupiter Merodach
Zib[14] Dele-bat Venus Ištar
Lu-lim Lu-bat-sag-uš Saturn Nirig (acc. to Jensen)
Bibbu Lubat-gud Mercury Nebo
Simutu Muštabarru Mars Nergal
mûtanu

All the above names of planets have the prefix of divinity, but in other

14 This is apparently a Sumerian dialectic form, the original word having seemingly been Zig.

inscriptions the determinative prefix is that for "star," /kakkabu/.

[*] This is apparently a Sumerian dialectic form, the original word having seemingly been Zig.

Moon and Sun.

Unfortunately, all the above identifications of the planets with the deities in the fourth column are not certain, namely, those corresponding with Saturn, Mercury, and Mars. With regard to the others, however, there is no doubt whatever. The reason why the moon is placed before the sun is that the sun, as already explained, was regarded as his son. It was noteworthy also that the moon was accredited with two other offspring, namely, Mâšu and Mâštu—son and daughter respectively. As /mâšu/ means "twin," these names must symbolize the two halves, or, as we say, "quarters" of the moon, who were thus regarded, in Babylonian mythology, as his "twin children."

Jupiter and Saturn.

Concerning Jupiter, who is in the above called Dapinu (Semitic), and Umun-sig-êa (Sumerian), it has already been noted that he was called Nibiru—according to Jensen, Merodach as he who went about among the stars "pasturing" them like sheep, as stated in the Babylonian story of the Creation (or Bel and the Dragon). This is explained by him as being due to the comparatively rapid and extensive path of Jupiter on the ecliptic, and it would seem probable that the names of Saturn, /Kâawanu/ and /Sag-uš/ (the former, which is Semitic Babylonian, meaning "steadfast," or something similar, and the latter, in Sumerian, "head-firm" or "steadfast"—"phlegmatic"), to all appearance indicate in like manner the deliberation of his movements compared with those of the planet dedicated to the king of the gods.

Venus at sunrise and sunset.

A fragment of a tablet published in 1870 gives some interesting particulars concerning the planet Venus, probably explaining some as yet unknown mythological story concerning her. According to this, she was a female at sunset, and a male at sunrise; Ištar of Agadé (Akad or Akkad) at sunrise, and Ištar of Erech at sunset: Ištar of the stars at sunrise, and the lady of the gods at sunset.

And in the various months.

Ištar was identified with Nin-si-anna in the first month of the year (Nisan = March-April), with the star of the bow in Ab (August-September), etc. In Sebat (January-February) she was the star of the water-channel, Ikû, which was Merodach's star in Sivan (May-June), and in Marcheswan her star was Rabbu, which also belonged to Merodach in the same month. It will thus be seen, that Babylonian astronomy is far from being as clear as would be desired, but doubtless many difficulties will disappear when further inscriptions are available.

Stars identified with Merodach.

The same fragment gives the celestial names of Merodach for every month of the year, from which it would appear, that the astrologers called him Umun-sig-êa in Nisan (March-April), Dapinu in Tammuz (June-July), Nibiru in Tisri (September-October), Šarru (the star Regulus), in Tebet (December-January), etc. The first three are names by which the planet Jupiter was known.

As for the planets and stars, so also for the constellations, which are identified with many gods and divine beings, and probably contain references, in their names and descriptions, to many legends. In the sixth tablet of the Creation-series, it is related of Merodach that, after creating the heavens and the stations for Anu, Bêl, and Ae,

> "He built firmly the stations of the great gods—
> Stars their likeness—he set up the /Lumali/,
> He designated the year, he outlined the (heavenly) forms.
> He set for the twelve months three stars each,
> From the day when the year begins, . . . for signs."

As pointed out by Mr. Robert Brown, jr., who has made a study of these things, the "three stars" for each month occur on one of the remains of planispheres in the British Museum, and are completed by a tablet which gives them in list-form, in one case with explanations. Until these are properly identified, however, it will be impossible to estimate their real value. The signs of the Zodiac, which are given by another tablet, are of greater interest, as they are the originals of those which are in use at the present time:—

Month Sign Equivalent

Nisan (Mar.-Apr.) The Laborer The Ram
Iyyar (Apr.-May) /Mulmula/ and the Bull of heaven The Bull
Sivan (May-June) /Sib-zi-anna/ and the great Twins The Twins
Tammuz (June-July) /Allul/ or /Nagar/ The Crab
Ab (July.-Aug.) The Lion (or dog) The Lion
Elul (Aug.-Sep.) The Ear of corn(?) The ear of Corn (Virgo)
Tisri (Sep.-Oct.) The Scales The Scales
Marcheswan (Oct.-Nov.) The Scorpion The Scorpion
Chisleu (Nov.-Dec.) /Pa-bil-sag/ The Archer
Tebet (Dec.-Jan.) /Sahar-maš/, the Fish-kid The Goat
Sebat (Jan.-Feb.) /Gula/ The Water-bearer
Adar (Feb.-Mar.) The Water Channel and the Tails The Fishes

Parallels in Babylonian legends.

The "bull of heaven" probably refers to some legend such as that of the story of Gilgameš in his conflict with the goddess Ištar when the divine bull was killed; /Sib-zi-anna/, "the faithful shepherd of heaven," suggests that this constellation may refer to Tammuz, the divine shepherd; whilst "the scorpion" reminds us of the scorpion-men who guarded the gate of the sun (Šamaš), when Gilgameš was journeying to gain information concerning his friend Enki-du, who had departed to the place of the dead. Sir Henry Rawlinson many years ago pointed out that the story of the Flood occupied the eleventh tablet of the Gilgameš series, corresponding with the eleventh sign of the Zodiac, Aquarius, or the Water-bearer.

Other star-names.

Other names of stars or constellations include "the weapon of Merodach's hand," probably that with which he slew the dragon of Chaos; "the Horse," which is described as "the god Zû," Rimmon's storm-bird—Pegasus; "the Serpent," explained as Ereš-ki-gal, the queen of Hades, who would therefore seem to have been conceived in that form; "the Scorpion," which is given as /Išhara tântim/, "Išhara of the sea," a description difficult to explain, unless it refer to her as the goddess of the Phœnician coast. Many other identifications, exceedingly interesting, await solution.

How the gods were represented. On cylinder-seals.

Many representations of the gods occur, both on bas-reliefs, boundary-stones, and cylindrical and ordinary seals. Unfortunately, their identification generally presents more or less difficulty, on account of the absence of indications of their identity. On a small cylinder-seal in the possession of the Rev. Dr. W. Hayes Ward, Merodach is shown striding along the serpentine body of Tiawath, who turns her head to attack him, whilst the god threatens her with a pointed weapon which he carries. Another, published by the same scholar, shows a deity, whom he regards as being Merodach, driven in a chariot drawn by a winged lion, upon whose shoulders stands a naked goddess, holding thunderbolts in each hand, whom he describes as Zer-panîtum. Another cylinder-seal shows the corn-deity, probably Nisaba, seated in flounced robe and horned hat, with corn-stalks springing out from his shoulders, and holding a twofold ear of corn in his hand, whilst an attendant introduces, and another with a threefold ear of corn follows, a man carrying a plough, apparently as an offering. On another, a beautiful specimen from Assyria, Ištar is shown standing on an Assyrian lion, which turns his head as if to caress her feet. As goddess of war, she is armed with bow and arrows, and her star is represented upon the crown of her tiara.

On boundary-stones, etc.

On the boundary-stones of Babylonia and the royal monoliths of Assyria the emblems of the gods are nearly always seen. Most prominent are three horned tiaras, emblematic, probably, of Merodach, Anu, and Bêl (the older). A column ending in a ram's head is used for Êa or Ae, a crescent for Sin or Nannar, the moon-god; a disc with rays for Šamaš, the sun-god; a thunderbolt for Rimmon or Hadad, the god of thunder, lightning, wind, and storms; a lamp for Nusku, etc. A bird,

61

perhaps a hawk, stood for Utu-gišgallu, a deity whose name has been translated "the southern sun," and is explained in the bilingual inscriptions as Šamaš, the sun-god, and Nirig, one of the gods of war. The emblem of Gal-alim, who is identified with the older Bêl, is a snarling dragon's head forming the termination of a pole, and that of Dun-ašaga is a bird's head similarly posed. On a boundary-stone of the time of Nebuchadnezzar I., about 1120 B.C., one of the signs of the gods shows a horse's head in a kind of shrine, probably the emblem of Rimmon's storm-bird, Zû, the Babylonian Pegasus.

Other divine figures.

One of the finest of all the representations of divinities is that of the "Sun-god-stone," found by Mr. Hormuzd Rassam at Abu-habbah (the ancient Sippar), which was one of the chief seats of his worship. It represents him, seated in his shrine, holding in his hand a staff and a ring, his usual emblems, typifying his position as judge of the world and his endless course. The position of Merodach as sun-god is confirmed by the small lapis-lazuli relief found by the German expedition at the mound known as Amran ibn 'Ali, as he also carries a staff and a ring, and his robe is covered with ornamental circles, showing, in all probability, his solar nature. In the same place another small relief representing Rimmon or Hadad was found. His robe has discs emblematic of the five planets, and he holds in each hand a thunderbolt, one of which he is about to launch forth. Merodach is accompanied by a large two-horned dragon, whilst Hadad has a small winged dragon, typifying the swiftness of his course, and another animal, both of which he holds with cords.

Excavations at Nineveh

An Assyrian

CHAPTER V

THE DEMONS: EXORCISMS AND CEREMONIES

Good and evil spirits, gods and demons, were fully believed in by the Babylonians and Assyrians, and many texts referring to them exist. Naturally it is not in some cases easy to distinguish well between the special functions of these supernatural appearances which they supposed to exist, but their nature is, in most cases, easily ascertained from the inscriptions.

To all appearance, the Babylonians imagined that spirits resided everywhere, and lay in wait to attack mankind, and to each class, apparently, a special province in bringing misfortune, or tormenting, or causing pain and sickness, was assigned. All the spirits, however, were not evil, even those whose names would suggest that their character was such—there were good "liers in wait," for instance, as well as evil ones, whose attitude towards mankind was beneficent.

The /utukku/. This was a spirit which was supposed to do the will of Anu, the god of the heavens. There was the /utukku/ of the plain, the mountains, the sea, and the grave.

The /âlû/. Regarded as the demon of the storm, and possibly, in its origin, the same as the divine bull sent by Ištar to attack Gilgameš, and killed by Enki-du. It spread itself over a man, overpowering him upon his bed, and attacking his breast.

The /êdimmu/. This is generally, but wrongly, read /êkimmu/, and translated "the seizer," from /êkemu/, "to seize." In reality, however, it was an ordinary spirit, and the word is used for the wraiths of the departed. The "evil /êdimmu/" was apparently regarded as attacking the middle part of a man.

The /gallu/. As this word is borrowed from the Sumerian /galla/, which has a dialectic form, /mulla/, it is not improbable that it may be connected with the word /mula/, meaning "star," and suggesting something which is visible by the light it gives—possibly a will-o'-the-wisp,—though others are inclined to regard the word as being connected with /gala/, "great." In any case, its meaning seems to have become very similar to "evil spirit" or "devil" in general, and is an epithet applied by the Assyrian king Aššur-bani-âpli to Te-umman, the Elamite king against whom he fought.

The **/îlu limnu/**, "evil god," was probably originally one of the deities of Tiawath's brood, upon whom Merodach's redemption had had no effect.

The **/rabisu/** is regarded as a spirit which lay in wait to pounce upon his prey.

The **/labartu/**, in Sumerian /dimme/, was a female demon. There were seven evil spirits of this kind, who were apparently regarded as being daughters of Anu, the god of the heavens.

The **/labasu/**, in Sumerian /dimmea/, was apparently a spirit which overthrew, that being the meaning of the root from which the word comes.

The **/âhhazu/**, in Sumerian /dimme-kur/, was apparently so called as "the seizer," that being the meaning indicated by the root.

The **/lilu/**, in Sumerian /lila/, is generally regarded as "the night-monster," the word being referred to the Semitic root /lîl/ or /layl/, whence the Hebrew /layil/, Arabic /layl/, "night." Its origin, however, is Sumerian, from /lila/, regarded as meaning "mist." To the word /lilu/ the ancient Babylonians formed a feminine, /lilîthu/, which entered the Hebrew language under the form of /lilith/, which was, according to the rabbins, a beautiful woman, who lay in wait for children by night. The /lilu/ had a companion who is called his handmaid or servant.

The **/namtaru/** was apparently the spirit of fate, and therefore of greater importance than those already mentioned. This being was regarded as the beloved son of Bêl, and offspring of /Ereš-ki-gal/ or Persephone, and he had a spouse named /Huš-bi-šaga/. Apparently he executed the instructions given him concerning the fate of men, and could also have power over certain of the gods.

The **/šêdu/** were apparently deities in the form of bulls. They were destructive, of enormous power, and unsparing. In a good sense the /šêdu/ was a protecting deity, guarding against hostile attacks. Erech and the temple Ê-kura were protected by spirits such as these, and to one of them Išum, "the glorious sacrificer," was likened.

The **/lamassu/**, from the Sumerian /lama/, was similar in character to the /šêdu/, but is thought to have been of the nature of a colossus—a winged man-headed bull or lion. It is these creatures which the kings placed at the sides of the doors of their palaces, to protect the king's footsteps. In early Babylonian times a god named Lama was one of the most popular deities of the Babylonian pantheon.

Lilith - Adam's First Wife

A specimen incantation.

Numerous inscriptions, which may be regarded as dating, in

their origin, from about the middle of the third millennium before Christ, speak of these supernatural beings, and also of others similar. One of the most perfect of these inscriptions is a large bilingual tablet of which a duplicate written during the period of the dynasty of Hammurabi (before 2000 B.C.) exists, and which was afterwards provided with a Semitic Babylonian translation. This inscription refers to the evil god, the evil /utukku/, the /utukku/ of the plain, of the mountain, of the sea, and of the grave; the evil /šêdu/, the glorious /âlû/, or divine bull, and the evil unsparing wind. There was also that which takes the form of a man, the evil face, the evil eye, the evil mouth, the evil tongue, the evil lip, the evil breath; also the afflicting /asakku/ (regarded as the demon of fever), the /asakku/ which does not leave a man: the afflicting /namtaru/ (fate), the severe /namtaru/, the /namtaru/ which does not quit a man. After this are mentioned various diseases, bodily pains, annoyances, such as "the old shoe, the broken shoe-lace, the food which afflicts the body of a man, the food which turns in eating, the water which chokes in drinking," etc. Other things to be exorcised included the spirit of death, people who had died of hunger, thirst, or in other ways; the handmaid of the /lilu/ who had no husband, the prince of the /lilu/ who had no wife, whether his name had been recorded or unrecorded.

The method of exorcising the demons causing all these things is curious. White and black yarn was spun, and fastened to the side and canopy of the afflicted person's bed—the white to the side and the top or canopy, the black to the left hand—and then, apparently, the following words were said:—

"Evil /utukku/, evil /âlû/, evil /êdimmu/, evil /gallu/, evil god, evil /rabisu/, /labartu/, /labasu/, /âhhazu/, /lilu/, /lilithu/, handmaid of /lilu/, sorcery, enchantment, magic, disaster, machination which is not good—may they not set their head to his head, their hand to his hand, their foot to his foot—may they not draw near. Spirit of heaven, mayest thou exorcise, spirit of earth, mayest thou exorcise."

But this was only the beginning of the real ceremony. The god Asari-alim-nunna (Merodach), "eldest son of Êridu," was asked to wash him in pure and bright water twice seven times, and then would the evil lier-in-wait depart, and stand aside, and a propitious /šêdu/ and a propitious

/labartu/ reside in his body. The gates right and left having been thus, so to say, shut close, the evil gods, demons, and spirits would be unable to approach him, wherever he might be. "Spirit of heaven, exorcise, spirit of earth, exorcise." Then, after an invocation of Êrêš-ki-gal and Išum, the final paragraph was pronounced:—

> "The afflicted man, by an offering of grace
> In health like shining bronze shall be made bright.
> As for that man,
> Šamaš shall give him life.
> Merodach, first-born son of the Abyss,
> It is thine to purify and glorify.
> Spirit of heaven, mayest thou exorcise, spirit of
> earth, mayest thou exorcise."

Rites and ceremonies.

As may be expected, the Babylonians and Assyrians had numerous rites and ceremonies, the due carrying out of which was necessary for the attainment of the grace demanded, or for the efficacy of the thanks tendered for favors received.

Perhaps the oldest ceremony recorded is that which Ut-napištim, the Chaldæan Noah, made on the /zikkurat/ or peak of the mountain after the coming forth from the ship which had saved him and his from the Flood. The Patriarch's description of this ceremony is short:—

> "I sent forth to the four winds, I poured out a libation
> I made an offering on the peak of the mountain:
> Seven and seven I set incense-vases there,
> Into their depths I poured cane, cedar, and scented wood(?).
> The gods smelled a savor,
> The gods smelled a sweet savor,
> The gods gathered like flies over the sacrificer."

Following in the footsteps of their great progenitor, the Babylonians and Assyrians became a most pious race, constantly rendering to their gods the glory for everything which they succeeded in bringing to a successful issue. Prayer, supplication, and self-abasement before their gods seem to have been with them a duty and a pleasure:—

"The time for the worship of the gods was my heart's delight,
     The time of the offering to Ištar was profit and riches,"

sings Ludlul the sage, and all the people of his land were one with him in that opinion.

It is noteworthy that the offering of the Chaldæan Noah consisted of vegetable produce only, and there are many inscriptions referring to similar bloodless sacrifices, and detailing the ritual used in connection therewith. Sacrifices of animals, however, seem to have been constantly made—in any case, offerings of cattle and fowl, in list-form, are fairly numerous. Many a cylinder-seal has a representation of the owner bringing a young animal—a kid or a lamb—as an offering to the deity whom he worshiped, and in the inscriptions the sacrifice of animals is frequently referred to. One of the bilingual texts refers to the offering of a kid or some other young animal, apparently on behalf of a sick man. The text of this, where complete, runs as follows:—

"The fatling which is the 'head-raiser' of mankind—
He has given the fatling for his life.
He has given the head of the fatling for his head,
He has given the neck of the fatling for his neck,
He has given the breast of the fatling for his breast."

Whether human sacrifices were common or not is a doubtful point. Many cylinder-seals exist in which the slaying of a man is depicted, and the French Assyriologist Menant was of opinion that they represented a human offering to the gods. Hayes Ward, however, is inclined to doubt this explanation, and more evidence would seem, therefore, to be needed. He is inclined to think that, in the majority of cases, the designs referred to show merely the victims of divine anger or vengeance, punished by the deity for some misdeed or sin, either knowingly or unknowingly committed.

n the Assyrian galleries of the British Museum, Aššur-nasir-âpli, king of Assyria, is several times shown engaged in religious ceremonies —either worshiping before the sacred tree, or about to pour out, apparently, a libation to the gods before departing upon some expedition, and priests bringing offerings, either animal or vegetable, are also represented. Aššur-banî-âpli, who is identified with "the great and noble Asnapper," is shown, in bas-reliefs of the Assyrian Saloon, pouring out a thank-offering over the lions which he has killed, after his return from the hunt.

Rebels being flayed to warn errant subjects.

CHAPTER VI

PROBLEMS WHICH THE STUDY OFFERS

Monotheism.

As the matter of Babylonian monotheism has been publicly touched upon by Fried. Delitzsch in his "Babel und Bibel" lectures, a few words upon that important point will be regarded in all probability as appropriate. It has already been indicated that the giving of the names of "the gods his fathers" to Merodach practically identified them with him, thus leading to a tendency to monotheism. That tendency is, perhaps, hinted at in a letter of Aššur-banî-âpli to the Babylonians, in which he frequently mentions the Deity, but in doing so, uses either the word /îlu/, "God," Merodach, the god of Babylon, or Bêl, which may be regarded as one of his names. The most important document for this monotheistic tendency, however (confirming as it does the tablet of the fifty-one names), is that in which at least thirteen of the Babylonian deities are identified with Merodach, and that in such a way as to make them merely forms in which he manifested himself to men. The text of this inscription is as follows:—

". . . is Merodach of planting.
Lugal-aki-. . . is Merodach of the water-course.
Nirig is Merodach of strength.
Nergal is Merodach of war.
Zagaga is Merodach of battle.
Bêl is Merodach of lordship and domination.
Nebo is Merodach of trading(?).
Sin is Merodach the illuminator of the night.
Šamaš is Merodach of righteous things.
Addu is Merodach of rain.
Tišpak is Merodach of frost(?).
Sig is Merodach of green things(?).
Šuqamunu is Merodach of the irrigation-channel."

Here the text breaks off, but must have contained several more similar identifications, showing how at least the more thoughtful of the

73

Babylonians of old looked upon the host of gods whom they worshiped What may be the date of this document is uncertain, but as the colophon seems to describe it as a copy of an older inscription, it may go back as far as 2000 years B.C. This is the period at which the name /Yaum-îlu/ "Jah is God," is found, together with numerous references to /îlu/ as the name for the one great god, and is also, roughly, the date of Abraham, who, it may be noted, was a Babylonian of Ur of the Chaldees. It will probably not be thought too venturesome to say that his monotheism was possibly the result of the religious trend of thought in his time.

Dualism.

Damascius, in his valuable account of the belief of the Babylonians concerning the Creation, states that, like the other barbarians, they reject the doctrine of the one origin of the universe, and constitute two, Tauthé (Tiawath) and Apason (Apsu). This twofold principle, however, is only applicable to the system in that it makes of the sea and the deep (for such are the meanings of the two words) two personages—the female and the male personifications of primeval matter, from which all creation sprang, and which gave birth to the gods of heaven themselves. As far as the physical constituents of these two principals are concerned, their tenets might be described as having "materialistic monism" as their basis, but inasmuch as they believed that each of these two principals had a mind, the description "idealistic monism" cannot be applied to it—it is distinctly a dualism.

And Monism.

Divested of its idealistic side, however, there would seem to be no escape from regarding the Babylonian idea of the origin of things as monistic.[15] This idea has its reflection, though not its reproduction, in the first chapter of Genesis, in which, verses 2, 6, and 7, water is

---

15 Monism. The doctrine which holds that in the universe there is only a single element or principle from which everything is developed, this single principle being either mind (/idealistic monism/) or matter (/materialistic monism/). (Annandale.)

represented as the first thing existing, though not the first abode of life. This divergence from the Babylonian view was inevitable with a monotheistic nation, such as the Jews were, regarding as they did the Deity as the great source of everything existing. What effect the moving of the Spirit of God upon the face of the waters (v.2) was supposed by them to have had, is uncertain, but it is to be noted that it was the land (vv. 11, 12) which first brought forth, at the command of God.

The future life.

The belief in a future life is the natural outcome of a religious belief such as the Babylonians, Assyrians, and many of the surrounding nations possessed. As has been shown, a portion of their creed consisted in hero-worship, which pre-supposes that the heroes in question continued to exist, in a state of still greater power and glory, after the conclusion of their life here upon earth.

"The god Bêl hates me—I cannot dwell in this land, and in the territory of Bêl I cannot set my face. I shall descend then to the Abyss; with Aa my lord shall I constantly dwell." It is with these words that, by the counsel of the god Aa, Ut-napištim explained to those who questioned him the reason why he was building the ship or ark which was to save him and his from the Flood, and there is but little doubt that the author of the story implied that he announced thereby his approaching death, or his departure to dwell with his god without passing the dread portals of the great leveller. This belief in the life beyond the grave seems to have been that which was current during the final centuries of the third millennium before Christ—when a man died, it was said that his god took him to himself, and we may therefore suppose, that there were as many heavens—places of contentment and bliss—as there were gods, and that every good man was regarded as going and dwelling evermore with the deity which he had worshiped and served faithfully during his lifetime.

Gilgameš, the half-divine king of Erech, who reigned during the half-mythical period, on losing his friend and counselor, Enki-du, set out to find him, and to bring him back, if possible, from the underworld where he was supposed to dwell. His death, however, had not been like that of an ordinary man; it was not Namtaru, the spirit of fate, who had taken him, nor a misfortune such as befalls ordinary men, but Nerigal's unsparing lier-in-wait—yet though Nerigal was the god of war, Enki-du had not fallen on the battlefield of men, but had been seized by the earth (apparently the underworld where the wicked are is meant) in consequence, seemingly, of some trick or trap which had been laid for him.

The gods were therefore prayed, in turn, to bring him back, but none of them listened except Êa, who begged him of Nerigal, whereupon the latter opened the entrance to the place where he was—the hole of the earth—and brought forth "the spirit (/utukku/) of Enki-du like mist." Immediately after this come the words, "Tell, my friend, tell, my friend—the law of the land which thou sawest, tell," and the answer, "I will not tell thee, friend, I will not tell thee—if I tell thee the law of the land which I saw, ... sit down, weep." Ultimately, however, the person appealed to—apparently the disembodied Enki-du—reveals something concerning the condition of the souls in the place of his sojourn after death, as follows:—

> "Whom thou sawest [die] the death(?) [of][16] ... [I see]—
> In the resting-place of ... reposing, pure waters he drinketh.
> Whom in the battle thou sawest killed, I see—
> His father and his mother raise his head,
> And his wife upon [him leaneth?].
> Whose corpse thou hast seen thrown down in the plain, I see—
> His /edimmu/ in the earth reposeth not.
> Whose /edimmu/ thou sawest without a caretaker, I see—
> The leavings of the dish, the remains of the food,
> Which in the street is thrown, he eateth."

It is naturally difficult to decide in a passage like this, the difference existing between a man's /utukku/ and his /edimmu/, but the probability is, that the former means his spiritual essence, whilst the latter stands for the ghostly shadow of his body, resembling in meaning the /ka/ of the Egyptians. To all appearance the abode described above is not the place of the punishment of the wicked, but the dwelling of

---

16 (?)"The death of the righteous," or something similar?

those accounted good, who, if lucky in the manner of their death, and the disposal of their bodies, enjoyed the highest happiness in the habitation of the blest. The other place, however, is otherwise described (it occurs in the account of Ištar's descent into Hades, and in the seventh tablet of the Gilgameš series—the latter differing somewhat):—

> "Upon the land of No-return, the region of . . .,
> [Set] Istar, daughter of Sin, her ear.
> The daughter of Sin set then her ear . . .
> Upon the house of gloom, the seat of Irkalla—[17]
> Upon the house whose entrance hath no exit,[18]
> Upon the path whose way hath no return,
> Upon the house whose enterers are deprived of light,
> Where dust is their nourishment, their food mud,
> Light they see not, in darkness they dwell,
> Clothed also, like a bird, in a dress of feathers.
> Upon the door and bolt the dust hath blown."

Seven gates gave access to this place of gloom, and the porter, as he let the visitor in, took from her (the goddess Ištar in the narrative) at each an article of clothing, until, at the last, she entered quite naked, apparently typifying the fact that a man can take nothing with him when he dieth, and also, in this case, that he has not even his good deeds wherewith to clothe himself, for had they outweighed his evil ones, he would not have found himself in that dread abode.

On the arrival of Ištar in Hades, Erêš-ki-gal commanded Namtaru, the god of fate, to smite Ištar with disease in all her members —eyes, sides, feet, heart, and head. As things went wrong on the earth in consequence of the absence of the goddess of love, the gods sent a messenger to effect her release. When he reached the land of No-return, the queen of the region threatened him with all kinds of torments—the food of the gutters of the city were to be his food, the oil-jars of the city (naptha?) his drink, the gloom of the castle his resting-place, a stone slab his seat, and hunger and thirst were to

---

17 One of the names of Nergal.
18 Or "whose enterer goeth not forth."

shatter his strength. These were evidently the punishments inflicted there, but as the messenger threatened was a divine one, they were probably not put into execution, and he obtained his demand, for Ištar was set free, receiving back at each gate, in reverse order, the clothing and ornaments which had been taken from her when she had descended thither. It is uncertain whether Tammuz, for whom she had gone down, was set free also, but as he is referred to, it is not improbable that this was the case.

WORKS BEARING UPON THE RELIGION
OF THE BABYLONIANS AND ASSYRIANS

Hibbert Lectures, 1887. The Religion of the Ancient Babylonians, by Professor A. H. Sayce.

The Religious Ideas of the Babylonians, by the Author, 1895 (Journal of the Victoria Institute, also separately).

The Religion of Babylonia and Assyria, by Morris Jastrow, jun., 1898. (German edition, vol. i. 1905, vol. ii. in progress.)

Babylonian Religion and Mythology, by L. W. King, M.A., 1899.

Gifford Lectures, 1902. Religions of Egypt and Babylonia, by Professor
A. H. Sayce.

The O.T. in the Light of the Records of Assyria and Babylonia, by the Author, 1903. (The portions referring to Babylonian Mythology.)

The Hymns to Tammuz in the Manchester Museum, Owens College, by the Author, 1904.

ARTICLES UPON THE ASSYRIAN AND BABYLONIAN DEITIES, AND
THE RELIGION OF THREE NATIONS, IN

Dictionary of the Bible, edited by Dr. James Hastings, and Encyclopædia Biblica, edited by Professor Cheyne.

www.ingramcontent.com/pod-product-compliance
Lightning Source LLC
Chambersburg PA
CBHW060205290526
45789CB00003B/1160